Arrivals and Rivals

A duel for the winning bird

Adrian M Riley

Brambleby Books

Arrivals and Rivals: A duel for the winning bird
© Adrian M Riley, 2007

All Rights Reserved

No part of this book may be reproduced in any form by photocopying or by any electronic or mechanical means, including information, storage or retrieval systems, without permission in writing from both the copyright owner and the publisher of this book.

978-0-9543347-9-6

Published 2004 by
BRAMBLEBY BOOKS,
Harpenden, Hertfordshire, UK
www.bramblebybooks.co.uk

2nd Edition 2007

Cover design and photo layout by Tanya Warren – Creatix
Cover painting by Deb Gillett

Printed in Germany for Brambleby Books by
AZ Druck und Datentechnik GmbH, Kempten

Dedicated to
the memory of Dr L. Roy Taylor (1924-2007),
a great lover of the natural world.

Contents

	Forewords	9
	Prologue	13
	Acknowledgements	15
Chapter 1	January – a moving experience	17
Chapter 2	February – getting into the groove	24
Chapter 3	Marching on together	40
Chapter 4	April – showers of migrants	47
Chapter 5	May – The Lochans of Mercury	52
Chapter 6	June and July – the half-time break	66
Chapter 7	August – unto the breach once more	75
Chapter 8	September – getting personal	96
Chapter 9	October – the Scilly season	113
Chapter 10	November and December – the final furlong	132
Chapter 11	The nineteenth hole	142
Chapter 12	Epilogue	146
Chapter 13	Further adventures of the Silver-haired Man	147
	The List	159

Foreword to the Second Edition

Following the success of the first edition of *Arrivals and Rivals* and the interest it engendered, both in birds *per se* and birding, and the fact that the book was generally well received amongst the birding community, the publishers decided that it might also be enjoyed by a wider readership. This belief stemmed from the fact that, although birds and the quest to see them in a competitive environment, framed the core theme of the book, then again the human element is always close to the surface of the central story…a story of rivalry yes, but also of human endeavour, strength and weakness in the face of stress. In fact, a remarkable tale about human endurance and hardihood.

In this new enlarged second edition, which includes an additional chapter and more colour photographs of birds (and some butterflies) he encountered on his birding expeditions, Adrian Riley re-tells the exciting story of his desire to see as many birds as possible in one year in the British Isles. Further, and in some ways more importantly, of the competition and enmity that this brought about from his rivals, especially one main rival, Lee Evans, a revered birder and (till then) recognised 'king' of the Birder-of-the-Year competition. Adrian removed him from this throne, albeit for one year only, and is pleased to tell us how he did it…and at what cost – physical, mental and financial.

But life does not stand still. In the additional chapter, he informs the reader of his enterprises since winning the birding 'trophy' in 2002. These include setting us his own natural history enterprise with his own website, as well as beginning and now completing a life's ambition – to write a field and site guide to all the species, subspecies and forms of the British and Irish Butterflies. Despite the fulfilment of this task, his competitive instincts are not yet satiated; as he says, "There are still all the dragonflies to photograph and report on"…as well as, no doubt, other branches of natural history as yet espied by his ever roving and accurate eye for detail. His genius is in showing us that however well a group of birds or insects has *apparently* been covered by others, there are still rich seams to be tapped, seams which reveal a wealth of biodiversity, interest and beauty...and which, as he stresses, must be preserved at all cost for future generations to also see and enjoy. Hence his continuing emphasis on, and commitment to, wildlife conservation.

Hugh D. Loxdale, MBE D.Phil.
Jena, Germany, November 2007

Foreword to the First Edition

Year-listing, the attempt to see as many bird species as possible in one calendar year, is a distinctive field of birding that most birders dabble in to some extent. Looking back at the size and composition of our species lists, we are able to gauge changes in our birding activity, our proclivity for twitching and relative changes in Britain's bird fauna, over the preceding years. As such it is an entertaining and informative way for birders to engage in friendly competition with our peers and, perhaps most importantly, with ourselves. However, there is a select band of obsessive birders who try to push back the boundaries of competitive year-listing and see as many species as humanly possible within one calendar year, travelling to every corner of Britain and Ireland to achieve this goal. This book describes the events surrounding one man's attempt to record the highest UK species total in 2002, and in so doing beat Lee Evans, the most obsessive year-lister the birding community has ever witnessed.

Adrian Riley's attempt to win the 2002 year-listing competition, and as a result deposing Lee temporarily from his position at the top of the year-listing tree, is the central theme of this book. Having said this, Adrian was determined to remain friends with Lee and the developments in their relationship as the year progressed form a fascinating backdrop against which the birding was played out. His book is therefore much more than just a birding diary but also an intriguing comment on the psychology of obsessive listing. Furthermore, running through the book are evocative descriptions of the many rare birds seen, beautiful images of the wild places visited and humorous accounts of twitching that all birders will recognize and enjoy. The book will therefore appeal to all birders and lovers of the countryside, as well as to those who want to know what makes obsessive birders 'tick'.

I was fortunate enough to accompany Adrian on many of the birding trips and twitches described in this book, and during this time we became very good friends. I also witnessed first hand the enormous level of stress that developed during the year, as the miles driven increased inexorably towards six figures and the opportunities to add new species inevitably decreased. However, as the pressure grew towards the end of the year, Adrian was indefatigable in his pursuit of new ticks. Having to hold down a full-time job, I was unable to join some of his trips and he was forced to drive alone overnight from Norfolk to such far-flung places as the Isles of Scilly and Scotland time after time. Understandably, the stress took its toll and he began to suffer doubts that he could continue until the year's end.

It is the rare birds that birders, who buy this book, will want to read about – because most of us, although we may look longingly at the plates of rare 'Sibes' and 'Yanks' in field guides, are unable to twitch everything at the drop of a hat or spend enough time in the field to find our own. Yet, we can get our kicks vicariously through reading about the exploits of those lucky full-time birders such as Adrian who can (and did) travel to Shetland and find his own Arctic Warbler, or fly to Fair Isle to twitch a River Warbler. But while I may be envious of the fabulous birds he saw without me, I take my hat off to his ability to keep going when, for financial and health reasons, he probably shouldn't have.

With his characteristic appearance – a shock of white hair and a Hamlet cigar never far from his lips (although he has since given up) – Adrian would have been a familiar sight to many birders in 2002, either on his Norfolk stamping grounds or at twitches from Shetland to the Isles of Scilly. Those who know him will recognize that he has the requisite skills to be an eminently successful birder and year-lister: immense patience and a compulsive desire to be the best at whatever he does. It was no great surprise therefore that he achieved his goal of winning the 2002 year-listing competition. But if you want to find out how his relationship with Lee evolved, then you will have to read this book – which I am sure you will enjoy as much as I did. He has already moved on to his next project, writing a site guide for all species and subspecies of British and Irish butterflies, and I await the outcome of this venture with great anticipation.

Jason Chapman, Ph.D.
Harpenden, June 2004

Prologue

Like so many birders, and particularly those trying to compile large year lists, the first morning of January usually heralds the start of a maniacal rush towards the pursuit of filling the pages of one's notebook. Norfolk, with its impressive flocks of wintering geese and other feathered magnets, is often the attraction for herds of twitchers eager to make a flying start to their collection of names. Their mindset is easy to understand for the world is full of those who love to collect. Many spend hours of their time seeking rare stamps, postcards, paintings or train numbers. However, the birder or angler is perhaps set apart from those worthy hobbyists by the fact that their particular quarry usually actively avoids discovery. It must be extracted from an environment over which it has domain and in which we are often strangers. Other genera of collectors can buy their desires at shops or at auctions with hard cash, whereas ours have to be hunted in the true sense of the word. Sadly, it is true that some twitchers seem not to appreciate the birds themselves and are motivated by the simple acquisition of 'ticks'. Even so, they must still develop the field craft, which is necessary to succeed. They must still hunt, and the bugle sounds the reveille on the first of January every single year. The year 2002 though, was to be very different for me.

For nearly a quarter of a century I had worked as a taxonomist at Rothamsted Experimental Station (now Rothamsted Research) in Harpenden, Hertfordshire. From within her bosom I ran the national moth survey and from there I grew from a raw and callow firebrat into (I like to think) a successful scientist with many publications to my name. Rothamsted is a wonderful institute, and I am proud to have been a member of staff there. I shall always be grateful for the opportunities she offered me and to my mentors – Dr Roy Taylor and Professor Brian Kerry (the latter, incidentally, an accomplished birder). But the time had come to leave. Ill health resulted in the taking of one final opportunity offered by my long-standing mistress – 'Voluntary Premature Retirement'. With Rothamsted's financial package and the proceeds of the sale of my house in Harpenden (a notoriously expensive town), I would buy a property in a cheaper area and invest for a modest income. Oh, how I hoped that I had done my maths correctly. My financial well-being and that of my wife Vanessa (Nessie) was in the balance. Oh yes, and I almost forget to mention: that 'cheaper area' was to be Norfolk. Not only is this the opening chapter of my story, but also the opening of a new and exciting chapter in my life.

Acknowledgements

By the end of the year, it became more and more obvious that this was a team effort. I may have been the one who actually went to see the birds, but without the following people, success would not have been possible and I am delighted to hereby acknowledge their help. To save any squabbling, I have listed them in alphabetical order.

Andrew, Tom, Chris and Dick at Rare Bird Alert for keeping me up to speed and help beyond my subscription; John 'Merlin' Bater for his support and encouragement and for being an 'ear' when I needed one; Richard 'Brommers' Bromilow for being eminently sensible and for suffering so many much-hated early mornings and changes of plan; Ian 'Dr Bugs' Burrows for his tactical awareness, ornithological expertise and support in a pursuit which I know he considers to be infantile; Pete Cambell and Paul Harvey for their advice on birding in The Shetlands; Jason 'Chappie' Chapman. What would I have done without you? Nessie aside, the most important piece in the jigsaw; Lee Evans for teaching me nearly everything I know about twitching; Bob Flood for making my birthday complete; Stuart 'City' Ford for being such a fearsome presence when the going looked like getting rough; Phil 'Grub' Gould for his wonderful sense of fun on all those long journeys; Les Holiwell and Adrian Webb for reminding me that birding could be a giggle; Paul Holmes for being the funniest companion of the year; Dave and Karen Leeming; Hugh and Nicola Loxdale for honing the manuscript; Alex 'Slim' McLennan for his down-to-earth approach and Anglo-Saxon sensibilities; John Pegden and Richard Bonser for being such sporting competitors; Vince 'Three lighters' Stewart for the occasional 'sub' and arse-kicking; Gary 'The Boiler'

Thoburn for tremendous support; Jonathan Tarry, my very own Chief Engineer 'Scottie', of Sculthorpe Service Station for caring so well for *The Enterprise* and Peter 'Penge' Thomas for huge help and companionship. Also, all my long-suffering friends at The Cross-Keys, Harpenden and The Horse and Groom, Sculthorpe – especially landlords Keith Charlesworth and Roger Samuel for their continuous support.

My deepest thanks are extended to Bernard Skinner for his willingness to share the fruits of his experience and wisdom.

January – a moving experience

After several years of early nights on New Year's Eve in order to rise before dawn for my usual birding drive to Norfolk, I promised my wife Nessie a traditional evening of festivity. Of course, this would involve enough alcohol to preclude driving anywhere the following morning (and longer than that if I had my way), but logic suggested there were no birds to be seen on that day that would not wait for the next. Ten o'clock on the 1st of January 2002 found me helping with scrub clearance on the local nature reserve at Batford Springs, near Harpenden, with my friend Richard Bromilow. The hard physical labour was good for my hangover, and I felt in fine spirits in doing something worthwhile. During a break from our toils, we ate some very welcome sausage sandwiches, and a Kingfisher delighted us with a sapphire and ochre fly-past. All was well in a world that would change dramatically for me over the coming months. Nessie not only got her traditional New Year's Eve but also a very jolly New Year's Day – the merriment lubricated by the oils of Harpenden's Cross Keys pub. Consequently, my car, an L-reg. Ford Escort, which I sentimentally nicknamed *The Enterprise*, sat lonely in space dock until the 3rd of January. This was clearly not a good way to start a birding year after telling everyone that I was going to try to win the annual competition to see the most species. Like Mohammad Ali, I was talking up a good fight; unlike him, I was not coming up with the goods.

By the 11th of January we were living in Sculthorpe, a small village on the outskirts of Fakenham, Norfolk. (On entering Sculthorpe, one can see the result of some wag's sense of humour who has made the 'c' into an 'o' which now reads 'Soulthorpe'. Does this mean a searching of the soul, I wondered?). Very quickly it became clear that Norfolk is a long way from many of the local sites that I used to frequent. It would be necessary to adjust my birding schedule to accommodate the fact that for the first week or so I would be based in Hertfordshire but not thereafter. Consequently, it would be financially astute to visit places around my present home before moving – not to mention those in Wales and the south-west of England. The journey to the Welsh choughs of Strumble Head, about five miles north-west of Fishguard, was simple from Harpenden, yet a long and awkward way from Sculthorpe. Moreover, there was the small matter of a Redhead (duck, not lady) on the way.

Kenfig, in south Wales, is a place I had never visited before, and what a shame the weather on the 3rd of January was so appalling. The wind that day was truly lazy and very rude. It barged its way straight through you, rather than having the good manners to go around. How much more cruel it was for my long-standing birding pal Jason Chapman who missed seeing the Redhead despite enduring the conditions for longer than was civilized. The bird was uncivilized too, as it seemed to possess the pagan ability to make itself slim enough to hide behind a single reed stem. Maybe this is why it was only the second one of its kind ever recorded in Britain. Although Nessie and I saw the dastardly duck, we hoped to have time to call back on our return journey to give Jason another chance; alas, it was not to be.

I respect Jason's abilities as a birder but, more importantly, I admire his eminently sensible attitude. Unlike one birder that I once met who sulked all the way home because he missed a bird and consequently ruined the day for everyone, Jason simply shrugs his shoulders and in his deep Welsh brogue makes his disappointment known – and then moves on efficiently and happily to the next bird. What good company he is, and how I wish that more were just like him. On this occasion, his perseverance was rewarded by a lugubrious Bittern, which I did not see, sailing over the reeds. Perhaps like the Bittern, I wish

Chapter 1

that I could say I enjoyed Kenfig but cannot, as the weather made it an altogether unpleasant experience. Unlike the bird, though, we had hot coffee and warm transport to escape that foreboding place. As I looked into my rear-view mirror I half expected to see it, sitting beside Jason on the back seat but, for reasons known only to bitterns, it preferred to stay behind. Did it too miss seeing the Redhead and needed to stay a little longer? One day I may go back and gain more favourable impressions but I doubt it as the desire is not there. Jason and I still argue about the merits of Kenfig, as he loves the place. It is the only thing we have ever argued about, and I suspect he will win in the end.

Strumble Head was altogether different. Instead of a skulking duck we were treated to Choughs, performing aerobatics amid a sunlit wind and below them the animated sea swarmed with gulls, auks and even the occasional stately Gannet. A Rock Pipit provided small brown interest. The journey home offered a Lesser Yellowlegs and an Iceland Gull, but fatigue amongst my travelling companions overcame my personal needs and ambitions. True, neither bird had been recorded for a few days and they may well have left, yet I felt sure this decision would be rued. Much later in the year it was, but at the time the welfare of my passengers had to come first. Jason and Nessie are not ones for birding regrets, and at that stage neither was I. How things were to change.

Looking back at my diary, I find it was several days before my next birding trip. My short-term memory never serves me well, yet if pressed, I'm sure I could find a convincing excuse for this lapse, and perhaps the impending move to Norfolk will satisfy the reader. Those of you who know Lee Evans will doubtless be aware of his boundless enthusiasm and energy. For several years I had been bewildered and bewitched by this and, when we met on the 11th for a day's 'local birding', even I was surprised by his intensity. We raced (as fast as *The Enterprise* could race) from site to site, gathering one 'year tick' after another; Hertfordshire one minute, Essex the next..., then into Suffolk. By the end of the day I was almost dizzy, but my notebook was full. At Lea Valley Park in Hertfordshire we saw two Bitterns and a Water Rail from the now famous bittern watchpoint, and at Abberton Reservoir in Essex there was yet another Bittern, Tundra Bean Geese and Bewick's and Whooper Swans.

Lee wasn't letting on at the time but he obviously had a specific goal in mind that day. For anyone present, it was a salutary lesson in how to achieve it, and I was a willing pupil. The roles of Master and Underling were clearly defined, and so I was very pleased to find a Ring-billed Gull that had eluded Lee in Suffolk. It was my only contribution aside from driving to exhaustion. Whilst at the Lea Valley Park, I watched Lee play with the Mute Swans that were begging for food, and it was obvious to me how much he loved birds. On that day I firmly believed that this is his major motivation in seeking birds and not the mindless acquisition of ticks of which he is often accused. The hungry white swans did not appreciate his games and they went away for the want of some bread.

Bedfordshire, Middlesex and Hertfordshire provided Nessie and me with their usual delights before our own personal migration to Norfolk. The Ring-necked Parakeets were particularly quarrelsome at Wraysbury in Middlesex; perhaps it was the fog, which was ever present that day and which also grounded several Red-crested Pochards, Smews and Goosanders at the Herts. and Middlesex Wildlife Trust reserve at Stocker's Lake. The latter three birds were not reported again as they presumably moved on. I wonder if our parakeets found peace too? Somehow I doubt it. These birds are maligned and mocked by many birders, particularly those who, with some justification, dislike the introduction of foreign species. To a degree I fall into this category myself: I particularly loathe introduced predators such as mink and domestic cats and also those huge submarine-like carp which now patrol so many of our lakes, canals and rivers. Small mammals, amphibians, birds and many of our native fish, such as Roach and Rudd, cannot cope with the predation and competition that these aliens bring upon them. However, perhaps hypocritically, I must say that I love the parakeets. They have a silliness about them which is similar to puffins but without the pathos of that species. They are comedians in the mould of the late Tommy Cooper (1922-1984) who would try so hard to be taken seriously but inevitably fail in the most hilarious way. They always make me smile on a chill January afternoon – 'Just like that!'

I hate shopping, especially when it involves indecision and parting with large amounts of money. A visit to a pine furniture shop with Nessie seemed destined for misery. We had by now moved to Norfolk, and domestic responsibilities were surely cramping my style. We had a house, but to create a home would involve the complete attention of both my bank manager and me. My patience was guaranteed; the bank manager's was not. Eventually, I ended up with a 'nice' kitchen and the sight of a few Bramblings at the same time. Nessie and I discussed our latest purchase over a stale cup of coffee and a fag in the shop's car park. Those Bramblings were certainly the most expensive tick of the year. As if to comfort me, a Lesser-spotted Woodpecker flew alongside the car on our homeward journey – homeward to Sculthorpe, not to Harpenden.

This new route was going to take some getting used to. Over the next few weeks, the adjustment became easier with sightings of all the winter specialities Norfolk had to offer that year. Taiga Bean Geese, Ross's Goose, a chip-eating Rose-coloured Starling and a Rough-legged Buzzard were now close to home and saved me a fortune in petrol. Shorelarks, Common Cranes, Snow Buntings and Barn Owls were by now becoming almost daily pleasures, and a King Eider at Wells-next-the-Sea provided an enigmatic diversion.

Of course, after living in Harpenden for nearly twenty-five years, homesickness and doubt were inevitably going to raise their ugly heads and I would be deluding myself if I said I was entirely happy at that time. I missed my local pub – The Cross Keys – and all its characters and I missed the relationships that had evolved over so many years. In birding terms, Lee had once suggested that I was 'The Boss' in Harpenden. I was not The Boss but there was now no doubt in my mind that I was 'The Catalyst'. One telephone call put things into perspective. I had just returned from a visit to a raptor-roosting point on Norfolk's north coast where I was delighted by Hen and Marsh Harriers, a Peregrine and a Merlin. I called Jason to relate my tale, and he was enthralled. On hearing the site was only fifteen minutes from my house, I believe there was uncharacteristic envy in his sigh. Few of my friends from Hertfordshire saw these birds as they no longer had someone to urge them to make the trip. Their 'Catalyst' had gone.

I am something of a 'technophobe' and pay little attention to the ever-shrinking world of electronic communication. Of course, I am aware of the Internet but, until recently, I thought it was a fancy piece of fishing equipment. I was equally certain the Worldwide Web was something to do with large spiders and that 'Dot Com' was a character in the TV programme *EastEnders*.

One phenomenon that did intrigue me though, was the Internet league table for year-listers on 'Surfbirds'. Apparently, my total for the year 2001 exceeded that of the top twitcher in the aforementioned league. If this year I was to 'go for it', should I take part in the public circus? The answer from Jason was blunt, persuasive and difficult to deny. Hence, I suddenly appeared on the scene as if a newcomer. From now on, Jason was to keep me updated with the entire 'going-on's' in what I was to discover to be a minefield of intrigue and egotism. At least I found out what had driven Lee so hard on our last day out. He claimed to have broken the calendar month record for the UK with 221 species in the first 31 days of the year. This was an astonishing achievement, which I doubt will ever be beaten and is testament to Lee's determination. Some doubted his integrity and, in return, he doubted theirs. In my naivety I was determined to remain friends with everyone – including him. Either way, it did little for my confidence and, for the first time, I was aware that I was playing with the big, bad boys. No more hiding behind the bike sheds with a crafty fag; no more lunchtime beers; it was 'game on'. My score for the month was a poor 164. I *was* 'the weakest link'.

February – getting into the groove

Of all years to pick in which to try and win the league it had to be the one in which Lee also had a bee in his bonnet. He knew about my retirement from Rothamsted and that I would be birding more or less full-time, but it would be presumptuous of me to suggest that this was his motivation for making such a flying start. I have spent many hours with him and I liked the man, have learned much from him and did not wish to analyse him. Having said that, I could not escape the feeling that the pupil was being given a sharp tap on the nose and, if he were to prove worthy, he had better show it in terms of results. Olive-backed Pipit, Goshawk, Golden Pheasant, Hawfinch and Woodlark made a quick statement of intent. The first of these was particularly satisfying, as I had never seen one before, and the views that Nessie and I had at Lynford Arboretum, Norfolk, on the 3rd of February were superb. It is an extremely scarce vagrant to these islands and an inland Norfolk winter specimen is a rarity indeed – on my new doorstep, too. The places from which the bird could be seen, as it pottered around in the grass, were few and far between, and I fear many people failed to see it at all. It remains one of the prettiest birds I have ever seen. The head markings are reminiscent of a Redwing, and the breast is spotted as beautifully as that of a Song Thrush. It had a charming demeanour as it searched delicately for its breakfast and, every now and then, it regarded us with a pleasant curiosity that bordered on amusement.

With such good fortune under my belt, I was hopeful of the right result later that day when my beloved Leeds United were to entertain the mighty Liverpool in a crucial Premiership game. On explaining this to a fellow birder at Lynford Arboretum, I was accused of being 'a sad bastard'. Part of his assessment proved to be accurate by mid-afternoon. Leeds lost four-nil and, in retrospect, it was the start of a decline in form which ultimately ended our European Champions League aspirations for the following season as well as our manager David O'Leary's tenure at the club. I don't blame the Olive-backed Pipit for all of this but I hoped it would bring me better luck than it did poor Mr O'Leary.

Many people hope one day to find something really rare: a valuable antique, an undiscovered painting by an Old Master or, for us, a 'Mega' rare bird. On the 4th of February that day finally arrived for me, or at least I thought it had. Flying over the A1065 just south of Swaffham was a female Goshawk. Nessie and I stopped and began searching for her. A large raptor was perched in a nearby pine tree and, although it was not our Goshawk, it was also not obviously anything we had seen before. It was large and buzzard-like but, although seemingly a *Buteo* species, was not a Common Buzzard. On our approach the bird took off and, as it flew low over my head, I could see that it had a conspicuously red tail. Yes, that's right, red! Apart from those towed along by Red Kites, I had never seen such a tail, and an intense sense of confusion, excitement and elevated body heat washed over me. In the meantime, the bird was lost from sight, but Nessie and I had sufficiently good views to put together the observational notes required to identify it and to convince the no-doubt sceptical birding world of our fantastic discovery.

What does one do in such a situation? By the time the alarm is raised the bird could be miles away, but I could not release the news straight away because I did not know what the news was. *The Enterprise* on-board library is not extensive; in fact, at that time, it comprised one book. Excellent though the *Collins Bird Guide* is, it did not include an illustration of our new bird. The nearest candidate was the Steppe Buzzard (which, I supposed, may have arrived on the same recent easterly weather which gave us the Olive-backed Pipit), yet my taxonomic instinct said quietly 'No'.

We rushed homewards, more speedily than was perhaps advisable (but always within the speed limits, Officer), towards the indigestible, though comprehensive *Birds of the Western Palaearctic*. A niggling doubt was brewing like a sultry thunderstorm at the back of my mind and, like the bird, I could not identify it. A little voice was saying, 'Remember the White-tailed Eagle.' But why?

At Nessie's suggestion, I phoned my friend, fellow Sculthorpe resident and excellent ornithologist, Ian Burrows. This did the trick. The previous year had indeed seen a 'White-tail' at Cockley Cley, a short distance from our sighting. As I was reminded of this, the penny dropped. It was accompanied by an escaped American Red-tailed Hawk that clearly was still in the area. Foolish I may have been but I still enjoyed the rush of adrenaline that came with it.

Fortunately, I have the ability to laugh at myself and this I did willingly. I was also pleased with the way I had conducted myself. The lesson to be learned here is to be certain of what you've seen before you inform everyone else.

February has traditionally been a busy birding month for me. It is the second half of my first target period (I split the year into sections containing 'must get' target species) and involves not only catching up with those common species missing from the late winter list, but also my first visit of the year to Scotland. This Scottish weekend is stamina-draining but rewarding, and I often do it alone. However, this year both Jason and my entomological partner-in-crime, Phil Gould, decided to come along: Phil because he simply loves to travel and Jason for the prospect of many new birds for his 'life list'.

Jason's year list had already got off to a racing start during a weekend in Devon and Cornwall where we saw Ross's and Bonaparte's Gulls and a Cirl Bunting. The Ross's Gull looked decidedly unhappy to me (there was something 'mucky' about its eyes), whereas the Bonaparte's Gull, of which we had almost tactile views, was perfectly proportioned and a delight to behold. A Mediterranean Gull also graced us with its presence, but we both missed out on a drake Ring-necked Duck that would have capped a great weekend. We accused each other of being bad talismans as, although we had individually seen the species many times, we had never done so together.

And so to Scotland. From Sculthorpe to Caerlaverock is one hell of a long drive, though such a journey is made that much easier by travelling overnight. Firstly, it avoids all of those irritating road users who inevitably get in the way of the busy birder. Secondly, it gets one on site at first light – an advantage that I habitually seek.

We set off at about 11.00 p.m. and, as we speculated upon what would be the first rare bird of the trip, I jokingly mentioned the White Stork that had taken up residence at Findern, near Derby. My compatriots pointed out that the night was pitch-black and still would be when we reached the area. Even so, I remembered Lee's solution to this very problem when he was hopeful of finding a Snowy Owl at Felixstowe the previous year – a *big* torch. When I packed my big torch for this trip, it was in anticipation of mechanical mishap in the Scottish mountains rather than the hair-brained pursuit of a roosting stork. The extended period of silence in the car suggested to me that my stupid idea was being considered seriously – which surprised me somewhat, as both Jason and Phil are scientists and should have known better. It seems though, that they were merely pondering the state of my mental health, and my brainchild was put to bed with the tenderness designed not to upset its eccentric father's sensibilities.

As the night ran away from the encroaching Scottish dawn, we became aware of the geese of Caerlaverock calling in the distance. The non-birder in our midst identified them before

February – getting into the groove

Jason and I even had time to rub the sleep from our eyes, as his family had for many years kept Barnacle Geese in captivity. Very soon it became clear that we were in the presence of thousands of these birds that flew noisily from roosting to feeding grounds. In the Norfolk goose flocks there is often a self-conscious 'Barney', but to see such herds of genuine winter visitors enjoying our shores is a true spectacle. For sure, Pink-footed Geese outweigh them, Taiga Bean Geese are rarer and to some Red-breasted Geese are more beautiful, but Barnacle Geese are just so…well…pretty. These were not to be the last geese of note either, for, within a couple of hours, several Greenland White-fronted Geese were in the sights of our binoculars at Loch Ken. Unfortunately, they were all in flight and their taxonomic features could not be studied – a cause of disgruntlement for my colleagues, although, as I had often watched them in the past, I was happy to regard the sighting as merely another year tick.

Was my attitude changing? Was I becoming more ruthless? In dark places where I did not particularly want to look I felt unfamiliar rumblings. Perhaps it was Phil's breakfast of tuna and pasta salad, which, I am sure, was medically dead by at least twenty-four hours. A very friendly local ranger showed us some stunning photographs of Red Kites (a species which was now, unbeknown to us, resident in the area) but, try as we might, we could not find them. It seems we were standing in the middle of yet another successful kite introduction scheme, and I wondered how long it would be before this species became once again a common sight throughout Great Britain. It is amazing to consider now that these fine birds were a common breeding species in seventeenth-century London. Apparently, they were then protected as useful scavengers at open refuse tips. Of course, that function has now passed but so too has much of the ignorant persecution that followed. We can only speculate on the future of this magnificent creature, as it wheels above the lands that its ancestors knew so well but fortunately it seems bright and hopeful.

Two rare ducks were our next targets: a drake American Wigeon had been present for some time at Loch Martnaham and a drake Green-winged Teal at Warwickdale Marsh. The two sites were conveniently close to each other in Ayrshire and would provide a profitable punctuation mark in our journey through Glasgow towards the gulls at Millichen Flood. Profitable it may have been, since I was fortunate enough to find both species; enjoyable it was not.

Loch Martnaham is situated in an agricultural landscape as far removed from one's idea of the Scottish wilderness as one might wish. The weather was fierce; a stiff cold wind carried with it biting icy rain, and underfoot the mud was adhesive and treacherous. The wigeon was fast asleep and intended to stay that way. Once or twice he raised his head to peer regretfully at being there and then went back to his dreams of warmer climes and lady American Wigeons. A pair of stately Smew – a good record for Scotland – was the only ray of sunshine. With a few expletives and high hopes for Warwickdale, we left the slumbering Yank to his fantasies. We should not have bothered. I liked the site very much, yet that awful wind and rain persisted for the duration of our visit. To make things worse, only I saw the bird. The many tufts of vegetation provided ample hiding places for a creature that did not want to be seen and this Green-winged Teal knew every one of them. With memories of Kenfig's demonic duck, Jason was losing his patience. At this point, the day was feeling long and anticlimactic; my colleagues were in particularly poor spirits as they had missed the Green-winged Teal, had only poor views of the American Wigeon and had got very wet in the process. Fatigue was also setting in, as this kind of weather is strength sapping – particularly as we had gone without quality sleep for so long.

Although I understood how they felt I was not succumbing to the same problems; my body was humming with anticipation.

I have also been blessed with good mental focus (some would call it obsessiveness) and I find these circumstances challenging rather than depressing. After only partial success with demisting the car windows, we gave up and pressed blindly on to Millichen Floods for Glaucous and Iceland Gulls. Both these species had been recorded there for much of the winter and were continuing to be seen on most days: surely our day would end on a high note, and the gloomy clouds that hung over Jason and Phil would disappear? It, and they, did not. There was no sign of any 'white-winged' gulls and the first leg of our tour was now nose-diving into a mire of despair and confusion.

Jason comforted himself with his first sightings of Scandinavian Herring Gulls (subspecies *argentatus*). They did not impress me in the least. It may sound arrogant, but I usually find it inexcusable to miss a bird as I always plan thoroughly, concentrate fully and apply myself completely to the job in hand. How then can I possibly fail? Well, like everyone else, I sometimes do. I still feel that my attitude is the correct one because when things do go wrong it is most constructive to look first to myself for the reasons why. I do the same when specimen Roach or Tench are my quarry and have always found it to be a good policy. In this way I feel that I am learning, rather than searching continuously for excuses. It is very easy to blame one's failure on the weather, tiredness or other people's behaviour and this is very definitely not constructive.

With these mantras of wisdom as my comfort, I complained about the appalling weather, moaned about what a long and tiring drive I had had, wished the guy in the bulldozer on the landfill site had knocked off early and then drove away empty-handed, satisfied that it was not my fault. I was cheered by the thought that we were now heading for one of my favourite places – Speyside. What wonderful memories I have of that place: a rogue Capercaillie chasing me through the forest, watching Crested Tits feeding young, marvelling at fishing Ospreys and repetitious drunken renditions of David Bowie's *China Girl* at Red McGregor's karaoke nights. Wonderful!

Scottish pub opening hours are a phenomenon, and it is very easy for the unwary to fall foul of the levity involved therein. Our stay in Grantown provides a salutary lesson. Realizing that 'normal' closing time was approaching, we downed our drinks and, in time-honoured fashion, ordered more so as to beat the bell. The bell did not ring, and hence the process was repeated. Still the bell remained silent. Like sharks in a feeding frenzy, we feasted on the unexpected bounty until our bellies were full. I have no idea what the hour was when we left but it was late enough to attract the attention of our friends in blue who were carrying a fairly loud bell of their own. Fortunately, we decided to leave before they decided to enter – that was where my luck ran out. A misplaced foot on a frozen step found me prostrate at the feet of a very large policeman. All of us were laughing so much – and he was so surprised – that we were given a brief moment in which to collect our thoughts. Jason used this time wisely and devised the cunning plan of asking the, by now smiling, Bobby if he was going to arrest us. Bizarre as it may seem, it worked, and we were sent on our way with no more than a good-humoured warning to behave ourselves. Being good citizens, we obeyed and headed back to our digs for a nightcap of the National produce (no, not haggis or porridge).

In 2001, Nessie and I found many Capercaillie droppings in the Caledonian pine forest near Grantown, but we could not locate the birds themselves. There was snow carpeting the ground and decking the trees like winter hanging baskets, and we were bewildered as to how a bird three feet long and as black as the ace of spades could evade detection in a white landscape. That experience shall forever remain a mystery to me and is probably puzzling to the reader. But surely, we three accomplished hunters could make amends. Like hell! The frustrations of the previous day were now turning into downright anger, and, as I have already explained, I find it constructive to direct these negative feelings at myself, thus generating the determination needed to succeed. There seemed to be nothing I could do about the apparently absent 'cappers', but our fortunes would change: of this I was sure. Missing the scarce and very localized species in the area would necessitate another trip and thus create a logistical and financial nightmare. Seemingly in fearful response to my renewed vigour, five crossbills came chattering into view. Ever argumentative, these birds are difficult to miss if they are around. Of course, the question of which species we had in our binoculars remained awkward and will probably do so for evermore. That they were not Common Crossbills was obvious from their calls; they were deeper in pitch and the 'attack' at the start of each '*tchup*' call was more urgent. There is much debate as to the specific status of the Scottish Crossbill, many authorities considering it merely to be a subspecies of the Parrot Crossbill. I am tending to favour this idea and so they enter my notebook as the latter. I think Lee is wise in referring to them as 'Scottish parrots'. Soon after watching the crossbills we heard the purring call of a Crested Tit from high in a pine tree. After much searching, we found the bird and were rewarded with some lovely views. Unfortunately, this was the only one we saw there and I pondered long on their apparent scarcity – a worry that I later discovered is shared by many. Predicted changes in global climate would surely affect such a species that maintains only a tenuous foothold in these islands.

Our luck was proved to be changing for the better by the news of five Waxwings at Aviemore. As we drove slowly into the town, Jason's sharp eyes caught sight of them in a tall, naked tree. It was very fortunate that he did spot them, as they immediately dropped from view into a small garden. There they commenced feeding on some apples that the owner of the house had impaled on the branches of a shrub. The only indication of the birds' presence was their trilling calls, which seemed to ooze contentment. Contented they surely were as they stayed in the garden until we left and would easily have escaped detection by other birders had we not telephoned the guys at *Rare Bird Alert* (RBA) with precise instructions on how they could be found.

A short drive took us to the RSPB reserve at Abernethy Forest. As we approached, I began to feel a familiar tingle of excitement for I love the place with all my heart. There is an ancient feel about it which envelopes you like a friendly old coat, and the silence here is almost visible; you can certainly hear it. Its creatures, too, seem primordial – the strutting 'Cock o' the Woods' (a wonderfully evocative old name for the Capercaillie), the delicate Red Squirrel and the Palmate Newts that somehow survive in the smallest of ride-side ditches. The verdant woods feel as bottomless as a mysterious green ocean, and when the winter snow falls I have actually heard the flakes kiss the ground as they land. Our short visit brought with it more wonderful memories, as we saw a male Capercaillie planing silently and expertly through the trees like a black ghost. Two Crested Tits gave a wonderfully comic show, and two Black Grouse completed our morning. As always, I was sad to leave, but at least we had many valuable ticks and a host of fantastic memories to take with us.

Our next port of call was the RSPB reserve at Loch of Strathbeg where we hoped to see a Snow Goose. I was particularly looking forward to this bird since I had never seen one whose credentials would stand close inspection. This one, I was told, was 'good'. On arrival, I went immediately to the visitor centre and watched the object of our desires take off with a heavy herd of Pink-footed Geese. Jason and Phil were visiting the 'Little Boy's Room'. The former just returned in time to see the goose before it disappeared from view; the latter did not. Riley's 'Rule Number One' states quite clearly that one should fill one's binoculars before emptying one's bladder. We tried

February – getting into the groove

until dark to find that bird, but it was not to be, and Phil left very disappointed. Leeds United lost again that afternoon and so I shared some of his misery. Exhausted and with the memories of Abernethy already fading away, we drove off. A lonely Woodcock bade us farewell.

To be honest, we hadn't seen much snow, and I was beginning to feel a little cheated, as it is surely an essential element of a Scottish winter. However, the following day found us in the high peaks of the Cairngorms Mountains near Braemar. Even here the snow was rather thin on the ground but there was enough to keep me amused while my two friends searched the mountainside for Ptarmigans, which I could see perfectly well from the warmth of *The Enterprise*. At first Jason and Phil appeared vaguely comical, but a snow flurry, carried by a wind strong enough to blow over my telescope, began to ring alarm bells in my head. These mountains appear benign, yet people die here every year and several personal close shaves (one with almost fatal consequences) have taught me to treat them with the utmost respect.

Fortunately, I was able to contact my friends by mobile phone and I advised them to come down immediately. Wisely they took the advice and were soon trying to warm up with lashings of hot coffee. In this they were unsuccessful and, despite their disappointment with the Ptarmigans, decided to leave the freezing mountains. Rarely have I seen two people so cold and never have I seen freshly cooked bacon and sausage sandwiches greeted with such glee. So engrossed were my companions with their food that they missed a Golden Eagle that appeared briefly over a distant ridge. So grateful were they for their breakfast that they seemed not to care.

Lower down the mountains we found a very odd-looking grouse, which had extensive black feathering on the mantle and conspicuous white markings on the wings and undertail coverts. A strange beast it was and it caused much conjecture. Phil managed to get a small image of it on film but, on trying to get closer, put it to flight. The familiar '*Rrrrrrr, go back, go back*' call suggested strongly that it was merely an aberrant Red Grouse. The mountains are without doubt beautiful but so unfriendly were they today that I was not sorry to leave.

A winter visit to Largo Bay, on the Firth of Forth, is always a joy. Many readers will know of the Surf Scoters that seem to be there every year; of course, their rarity invariably makes them prime targets. However, the sheer number of ducks, grebes and, if you are lucky, divers which can be seen makes this a special place indeed. This year, the Surf Scoters were found quickly amongst large flocks of Velvet Scoters and smaller numbers of Common Scoters. All three species were often close inshore and the taxonomic features of each could therefore be easily studied. In a previous year, I remember having one of each in the same field of view of my telescope. This year, Greater Scaup, Goldeneye, Long-tailed Duck, Common Eider and Red-breasted Merganser were all common; a few Red-throated Divers and a Black-throated Diver graced us with their presence, and lone Black-necked and Red-necked Grebes were the 'icing on the cake'.

We reported our findings to RBA and were treated to the aural equivalent of a 'raised eyebrow' in response to the news of Black-necked Grebe. This surprised me since I had seen the species there in previous years. It is a humble man who questions his own judgement and, at this point, I confess to feeling very humble indeed. It is true that most black-necked grebes overwinter in more southern waters. I am always prepared to accept that I may have dropped a clanger, but we were all sure our identification was correct.

After a truly disgusting 'Indian' meal in Northumberland, served by the most miserable staff and for which Scottish currency was apparently not acceptable tender, we decided collectively that the following morning I should ring RBA and re-state our case. This I did, along with news of the unexpectedly overwintering and delightful Hume's Yellow-browed Warbler, the skittish Siberian Chiffchaff at Newbiggin in Northumberland and the Ring-necked Duck at Low Barnes, Durham. I was gratified by confirmation that Black-necked Grebes do, in fact, spend time at Largo and that all doubts had been erased. I *knew* this was the case, so why on earth did I doubt myself?

In retrospect, I now see that this year was to be the most important of my birding life. My honesty, integrity, ability and physical and mental stamina were all up for public and self-examination, and I could simply not afford to fail in any department. It was only February, and already there was a dawning of this realization. No one else recognized it at this time. Few people outside my circle of friends knew who I was, and those who did had their own lives to live and saw the antics of birders, such as Lee and myself, as mere passing amusements.

Slowly, day-by-day, I was finding the game less and less amusing. In fact, I was beginning to understand that it was not a game at all. That particular day at Largo, with all its soul searching about my judgement, was a huge turning point, both in the year's birding and for me personally. Top class cricket batsmen always say that if you are going to slash at a ball wide of the off stump then slash bloody hard and it will clear the slip fielders. From now on, if I was going to call in a bird, the identity of which I was confident, then I would shout it hard from the rooftops – providing, that is, it was politically expedient to do so.

The Low Barnes Ring-necked Duck was something of a milestone. Separately, Jason and I had each seen the species on several occasions but time and time again we had returned home disappointed after joint trips. We broke that particular duck, if you will forgive the pun, shook hands in mutual smugness at having done so and headed south. Although Durham was still a long way from home, there was a pervasive 'end of term' feeling in the car and, as is often the case under such circumstances, our conversations were getting sillier and sillier. By now we really had had enough and were pretty well exhausted. Onwards we went, and I kept driving seemingly forever. By this time there were large gaps in my memory of the road gone by, although I was strengthened by my recollections of the drive last year to Balvicar's Snowy Egret. This tour was nothing by comparison, as I at least was allowed to sleep every now and then. The egret made me 'eat tarmac' for hours on end with little rest, and the journey prompted my travel companion Mike Thompson to call it 'an epic'.

I shall never forget the backslapping and self-congratulation on arriving home from that trip. I had never met Mike before yet, from then on, consider him a friend. Journeys such as these have little to do with birding; they are more about achieving something as a team. You encourage each other, keep each other amused, praise each other for past achievements, cajole each other when the goal seems out of reach and laugh together when you score. Towards the end of such odysseys one's thoughts become abstract, and I was by now beginning to relive the memories of Mike's dry Geordie sense of humour and mix it into a cocktail with the Monty Python sketches that were being rerun on the bridge of my *Enterprise.*

As captain, I had to concentrate the minds of my crew on finding the Great Grey Shrike of Leash Fen, Derbyshire. Our assignment was not even then complete since we had still to rendezvous with the notoriously thuggish White Stork of Findern. Leash Fen exploded the imagery to smithereens, as, on arrival, we were greeted by a sickening void that the shrike had once occupied. Morale sank to rock bottom – as it does when one takes a thunderous right hook in the dying seconds of the penultimate round. As with boxing, the bell sounds, you get to your stool, take on water, gulp in oxygen, drink up the freshness of the air. The bell sounds again, and you tense your muscles and fibres as you move heavily towards the centre of the ring – in this case ponderously towards the monstrous White Stork of Findern.

By now, the rain was falling in a steady drizzle and visibility was poor. The stork could have been hiding behind any one of the hedges or trees. We found the Great Field of Tyres, which was its castle, but it was not there. The rain blurred our vision such that its elusiveness became tenfold. We were cold, exhausted and hungry. Then, in a far corner of its kingdom, I saw it. Bespattered it was with mud, and the once fine feathers matted to greasy arrowheads. Its head hung low. It was as if our very gaze had dethroned it. For a while we watched through steamy 'scopes and, on realizing that it had not seen us, we left it with what dignity remained in its sorrowful frame. We were pleased that, with what weapons we had available, we did not need to use the big torch. With hearts both heavy and light, we made our way back to *The Enterprise*, and our thoughts turned to home. I needed a bath, I needed my bed, I needed a good meal but, most of all, I needed Nessie's smiling face.

The remainder of the month proved to be excellent for gulls. Nessie and I found Glaucous, Yellow-legged and Caspian Gulls at Fisher Fleet in Kings Lynn and the Iceland Gull over the rubbish of Lancaster Tip where everyone else seemed to be watching the mud of the nearby river. The surroundings may not have been salubrious, but the bird was a gem. Without doubt though, the star was the Ivory Gull at Black Rock Sands in north Wales – particularly as we missed the one at Fairhaven.

Some years ago, I kept and flew Cumulet Pigeons. This ancient snow-white Belgian breed is in danger of dying out through inbreeding and lack of fashionable favour. The Ivory Gull, with its perfect lines and chalky feathers, brought back many happy memories of my high flying and faithful beauties. That I relocated the Black Rock bird (to my astonishment no other birders were present on our arrival) added to the thrill and made up for misidentifying an aberrant Common Scoter as the much sought-after Black Scoter at Llanfairfechan. This particular faux pas made me feel a complete imbecile, but at least I admitted my mistake. I know that others present that day did not. Who was the bigger fool, I wonder? Norfolk saw the month out with a very stately but rather aloof Great White Egret and an arrogant Hooded Crow. As usual, the Cetti's Warblers were elusive at Wheatfen Broad but noisily recorded their presence there whenever asked to by the early spring sun. However, probably the most significant event of the month was my trip on the 21st with Jason and Phil.

Jason and I met Lee, among others, at a site in Bedfordshire which Lee has asked me not to disclose, where we were treated to fantastic views of Lady Amherst's Pheasant. From there we travelled to Thursley Common in Surrey and eventually enjoyed distant views of a Great Grey Shrike. Here we also met another well-known birder who told me knowingly that if I were to challenge Lee by trying to win this year's competition 'my name would be mud'. His comments made my stomach flutter like a swarm of migrating butterflies, and I was bathed in a sense of foreboding. Would Lee really speak badly of me? Surely not; after all we were mates. All the way to Dorset I worried about this. Even the Lesser Scaup at Little Sea seemed worried as it hid for most of the afternoon and then tried to be something else. The Dartford Warblers expressed their worry by buzzing unseen from the gorse bushes there. All the way home, I worried. I slept badly that night. I was still worried the next day. I finished the month with my total on a less than creditable 217 – still not even level with Lee's score for January. I worried about that too, but at least I was ahead of the rest of the field. I felt safe in second place.

Marching on together

March is the first anticlimax of the year. At least it usually is. The frenetic activities of January and February are over, and all the winter birds are safely gathered in. By now some, such as the Taiga Bean Geese, had already dispersed or left for their summer quarters, leaving the forlorn beet fields of Cantley and its like to the ghosts of winter past. They are welcome to it. The name itself would have inspired the late great Peter Cook and Dudley Moore, and no one but a birder on a wild goose chase would want to go there. I would rather go to Kenfig.

Mid-March is filled with anticipation, as the first spring immigrants begin to arrive. Towards the end of the month we may expect to hear the chaotic song of pioneering Sedge Warblers. Excitable Little Ringed Plovers and stately Garganeys begin to adorn our marshes and the first startled Stone Curlews stare at us to the languid music of Woodlarks from the desolate Breck district of East Anglia. It is our good fortune that these birds, or at least some of them, remain with us for the summer alongside the Swallows and House Martins whose breathtaking aerial mastery always thrills. However, for the twitcher it is their itinerant friends who are of more interest. What delights will accompany them on their journey? This year I was lucky enough to find Firecrests and Ring Ouzels on my local patches. I was grateful but not satisfied. My appetite was whetted rather than sated. A Serin at Sidcup in Kent helped yet it did not sing for me, and its choice of quarters was questionable – London waste ground is a far cry from the splendours of the Scottish Highlands. Distant views of a Lesser Yellowlegs were an inadequate reward for an overnight drive to the inauspicious Frodsham Marshes, and the fact that I could not find the nearby

Great White Egret made for a weary journey home. Still, these were good quality ticks, and my evolving lack of sensitivity was beginning to make me feel that this was more important.

I thoroughly enjoyed a trip to Devon though, where two ghostly Spoonbills emerged from the dawn at Bowling Green Marsh. This site near Topsham is a pure delight, as one can get marvellous close views of the waders that frequent it. I have never left disappointed and recommend that every birder spend an hour or two there should the opportunity arise. On the same day I managed to find the American Black Duck at Slapton Ley National Nature Reserve. This much-maligned animal, which someone once described to me as 'underwhelming', is in fact rather pretty. I think its delicate tones should be appreciated rather than mocked, but then 'beauty is in the eye of the beholder' and I was having a good day. It got better yet with a visit to Portland Bill, Dorset, where, braving the strong winds, I was rewarded with a Balearic Shearwater amongst a myriad of other seabirds, such as Gannets, Common Scoters and Guillemots. Those watching from the relative comfort of the observation station apparently missed most of the action as they were that much further from the sea. The adage 'no pain, no gain' comes to mind. I was now in excellent spirits for the journey home, which, thanks to a tip-off from one of the lads at RBA, was punctuated with a visit to Corfe Mullen, Dorset, to see an enigmatic American Herring Gull (then considered to be merely a subspecies of Herring Gull but now given specific status).

Gulls are not my favourite birds, and I find their taxonomy rather too taxing. However, a friendly birder pointed this one out to me, and I was assured that I would one day appreciate its significance. At the time, I was grateful but unimpressed. How right he was later proved to be! I arrived home pleasantly exhausted, had a couple of pints of cider and slept the 'sleep of kings'. But all the dreams I may have had that night were nothing compared with what Cornwall had in store for me later in the month.

Qualification for the European Champions League was now looking even less likely for my beleaguered Leeds United, and, after their splendid start to the season, I found this extremely frustrating. Also frustrating was spring's reluctance to arrive. It was leaking in rather than bursting forth, but secretly something big was brewing in the south-west. On the evening of the 24th, I received a call from Lee who, in no uncertain terms, insisted on a visit to Cornwall where there were 'loads of birds'. He was returning from an arduous trip to Scotland and so I agreed to drive. I picked him up that night, and there began the most remarkable birding weekend I have ever had.

By one o'clock that afternoon we had arrived at Nanquidno, West Cornwall, and, within half an hour, I was feasting my eyes on a stunningly beautiful male Black-eared Wheatear. I had never seen this species before and would have been pleased enough to find the relatively dull female or immature autumn bird. This individual, though, was perfect in its finest black and white livery. I watched it for several minutes before it honoured an appointment elsewhere, and we decided to move on to Porthgwarra. As we left, a tall and somewhat fearsome looking man strode up to Lee with what appeared bad intent. He raised his arm, and I dropped my 'scope. As he neared his quarry, I too moved nearer to protect it. That familiar buzzing started in my ears, which is a sure symptom of raised adrenaline levels. Then he reached out his spade-like hand and ... placed it in Lee's in an affectionate handshake. Sycophancy it may have been but even that was far better than my imagined alternative. On our way we went, leaving behind a large and happy man who had met his hero and a Black-eared Wheatear, which seemed to be the only one that knew whether it was 'eastern' or 'western' in subspecies. I suspect it cared little anyway. I know I didn't.

By two o'clock we were at Porthgwarra, standing near

something known as the 'Doctor's House'. Local birders would know what and where this is, but I imagine most visitors would be puzzled. For the record, it is a large house, presumably where a doctor lives or lived, just north-west of the car park. It has a large garden, which is attractive to migrating birds, and today it was host to perhaps the most exotic looking of visitors – a Hoopoe. I commented on what a nice bright bird it was, but Lee disagreed, saying it was '…quite dull'. A comedian standing nearby jokingly agreed and suggested it was '…of eastern origin and must have come in with the Black-eared Wheatear'. The Hoopoe looked on with dismay. It had surely never met the wheatear and probably never would. As the bird cocked its magnificent head towards mine, I wondered if we were sharing a joke at everyone else's expense. The weather was by now becoming inclement. Dark mist loomed, but undeterred we marched towards St Leven where Lee located a Woodchat Shrike whose splendour was only slightly bedraggled by the miserable conditions. What a sight it was to behold, with its chestnut crown and nape and snow-white wing bars. As it hopped inquisitively along the hedgerow it seemed to be looking for something more important than food. I think it was Spain.

Lee had 'got wind' of three Cattle Egrets which were reportedly in the area, but of which I knew nothing. Allegedly they were breeding amongst a local colony of Little Egrets and 'mum' was the word. Nevertheless, he told everyone he met of their presence, and so I feel no obligation now to keep this between ourselves. He had instructions as to their usual haunts, yet it took much searching and some possible trespassing to find them. Anyway, find them we did and we slapped each other on the back for our efforts. I wonder if they will return to that little corner of England and I wonder if they really will breed? I hope so but I doubt it. Nice story though, and, just in case you hadn't already, you may notice that I make no mention of the locality.

For my life I cannot remember why we decided to return

home at that point, but we did. The greatest prize in the form of a Scops Owl still remained. I believe a joint decision had previously been made to go home that same day, although I may be wrong. In retrospect, this would have been a crazy arrangement, though perhaps politically astute with a Norfolk-bound Nessie doubtlessly becoming ever more envious. We engaged 'warp drive' and off *The Enterprise* sped with its happy crew of two. We had reached Exeter when we received a 'Starfleet communication' telling us of the continued presence of the owl. There was nothing for it. Duty dictated that we must return to Cornwall. By midnight or thereabouts, we were in the car park at Porthgwarra. The bird had been seen shortly before but had since disappeared. All save one other birder had gone the same way, and Lee was decidedly edgy. On went the headlights over its favourite feeding ground. Nothing. Darkness for a while, then on again. Still nothing. It was then that I first realized that there was something a little unusual about Lee. 'Do you think it will show again?' he said.

'Yes,' was my reply.

'Really, really, you think it will show?'

'Yes, trust me, I'm sure it will.'

'Really? Oh, great!'

I felt like my grandfather must have done in 1972, when Leeds United played in the centenary FA Cup final against Arsenal. Shortly before kick-off, I asked if he thought we would win. 'On current form they should piss all over them,' he said. 'Really? Oh, great!' was that little boy's response. Leeds ran out 1-0 winners and collected their only FA cup-winner's medal to date. The owl showed, and Lee looked like I felt that day over 30 years ago. It became obvious to me that I was in the presence of not one but two lost souls that night. The owl looked decidedly ill with drooping wings and unsteady flight. Lee looked tired. Both looked vulnerable, and my heart went out to both of them. We watched the little creature for about an hour and a half, each

Chapter 3

taking turns to illuminate it with the big torch, while it skilfully emptied large worms of their bodily contents. This was morbidly fascinating for one such as myself who has an irrational terror of earthworms. Sated, our owl went off to rest, and so did we. Ever the birder, I wanted to count Cetti's Warblers the next morning at Marazion Marsh, and, as there is a car park there, this seemed the logical place to 'crash out'. In the midst of our sleep, Lee answered a phone that did not ring, and at dawn I told him I had counted five singing Cetti's Warblers, but he did not hear me or any of them.

Early morning found us back at Porthgwarra, where the Scops Owl was asleep in a sallow bush. I envied it, but at least Lee seemed refreshed and more like his usual effervescent self. I was beginning to feel 'cattle trucked' as a dear West Ham supporting friend of mine would say. Like the Grand Old Duke of York, of the ten thousand men fame, Lee *'...marched me up to the top of the hill, then marched...'* me off to St Just. Here at the second attempt, we had the most spectacular views of a Night Heron, which perched belligerently only a few yards distant. Several people from nearby houses came to see their curious visitor and were enthralled by the sight that lay through our telescopes. Lee is charming in such situations, answering everyone's questions with knowledge and infectious enthusiasm.

An Alpine Swift came up on our pagers. We set about and chased it and chased it. Lee used his knowledge of the local topography and acquired wisdom in trying to find the bird, but to no avail. I followed along not knowing what on earth I was doing, and then came a call on Lee's mobile to say that not one but two Alpine Swifts had been located near St Just. Immediately we went there and found them. They performed magnificently, reminding me of small Hobbies as they swooped and glided purposefully through the unresisting air. I sat on the tailgate of *The Enterprise*, trying to assimilate all I had seen over the last two days. 'Resistance was futile.' After a final visit to the Cattle

Egrets, we trekked home. How I made it back to Norfolk I shall never know but I did so and before closing time, too! I had seen so many fantastic sights over the previous two days that it would have been pointless to dream that night, so I slipped into something resembling a coma and stayed there contentedly for many hours.

By the end of March my total had increased to 243 species, and I was beginning to feel on top of my game. There were clearly now three 'horses' dominating the race – with myself, Lee and John Pegden some way clear of the rest of the field. It was pointless asking Lee for his total as he was reluctant to let on, but the lead at the top of the Surfbirds league was changing regularly between John and myself. John's performance was starting to concern me a little. I fully expected to finish second behind Lee at the end of the year, yet the dark spectre of third place now reared its ugly head. In my days as an amateur football coach, I would always tell my players to concentrate fully on their own performance and forget about that of their rival teams. The most important competition is that which you have with yourself. It was time for me to practice what I had been preaching. In the words of the former Leeds manager, Howard Wilkinson: 'There's miles of football left yet'.

April – showers of migrants

After a faltering start to the spring migration, April fulfilled its promise by delivering all of the commoner species which so brighten our English summers. The most treasured of these must be the warblers whose songs fill the shimmering air with lilting melodies, chattering mimicry and insect-like churring. Much of the month was spent searching my local coastal scrubland that stretches from Snettisham to Heacham in search of rarities such as shrikes, or perhaps a Hoopoe. During the many days when such birds were absent, I was heartened by the presence of so many warbling and buzzing friends. All were there: Willow and Garden Warblers, Lesser and Common Whitethroats, Chiffchaffs and Blackcaps sang their liquid love songs; Reed and Sedge Warblers gossiped in staccato chaos and several male Grasshopper Warblers lurked, usually unseen, in the brambles from where they claimed their territory like huge crickets. Wheatears were a regular sight but not so much, I was told, as in previous years. Yellow Wagtails, some of which glowed canary yellow in the bright sunshine, often delighted me. They always seemed nervous though, and difficult to approach. I was regularly finding Ring Ouzels and, on the 20th, I was amazed to stumble across a flock of seven of these magnificent Mountain Thrushes that '*tack-tacked*' their disapproval of my intrusion as they bounced from one hawthorn tree to the next.

I believe that, metaphorically speaking, lightening can sometimes strike twice in the same place. So when here, I usually visit a small pond where several years ago my friend Ian Burrows found a little Bittern. Unfortunately, I was not to be quite so lucky but once saw a pair of Garganey as well as a pair of Mandarins. On another day, during a violent storm, Jason, Phil and I were fortunate not only to avoid some very real lightning but also to witness a fall of migrating birds that included a Wood Sandpiper.

The Heacham to Snettisham area was proving very productive and searching similar habitats elsewhere in the county also paid dividends. A very secretive Long-eared Owl blinked briefly at me at Walsey Hill. Stiffkey Fen offered a Little Ringed Plover and the occasional Whimbrel that struggled noisily over the adjacent marshes, where the now fairly common Little Egrets would look on in apparent astonishment. The occasional Fieldfare remained at Horsey Dunes where, on one occasion, I was delighted by the incongruous sight of a fine specimen perched in the same stunted hawthorn as a Ring Ouzel. This at least compensated for the continued absence of Red-backed Shrikes.

On a trip to Horsey on the 26th, I almost crashed *The Enterprise* at the sight of an Osprey gliding over the A47 near Acle and I later popped in to see a ring-laden White Stork near there, which looked almost as forlorn as his 'King' at Findern. That day was rounded off nicely at Great Yarmouth cemetery with a Wood Warbler, whose curious song resembles a falteringly spinning coin on a sheet of metal.

My faith in Norfolk's coastal scrubland was handsomely rewarded on the 24th by a beautiful, if indignant, Western Sub-alpine Warbler. How I would have loved to find that bird myself. Ah, well, as they say in football: 'There's always next year'. One last reference to scrubland warblers concerns a Willow Warbler that spent a few days near Sculthorpe. The song of this individual was very strange, as the first half resembled that of a Chiffchaff. A few days after Jason and I discovered the bird, the rumour of the presence of a possible Iberian Chiffchaff started to spread. Having heard our bird, one can understand how this may have arisen, since the two are somewhat similar.

No major trips were planned for April and so the month was spent as described, with occasional days out to see the various national rarities reported by RBA. The longest of these trips was made to Llanfairfechan to put right my previous embarrassment at misidentifying the Black Scoter. I arrived at daybreak on the 2nd and was greeted by a picturesque dawn and our American visitor close inshore. I had little time to study the bird, as the tide was fast receding. Long enough, however, to see that the specimen I had seen previously was clearly not the same as the one now in my 'scope. After twenty minutes or so, it flew north with a few Common Scoters to join a larger flock over deeper water, and that was that. Before I left, a Black Guillemot presented a pleasant surprise, more especially as I did not realize this species occurred there. It also constituted a further year tick for my swelling list.

A very obliging Spotted Crake at Belvide reservoir, Staffordshire, a less friendly Kentish Plover at Oare Marshes, a Kent wildlife trust reserve, and a pretty Red-rumped Swallow at Hull provided only slightly less excitement. I had seen these species on several occasions before, yet their appeal was shrouded by the insidious mists of needing something very special and, better still, not shared by Lee or John. The Whiskered Tern at Cotswold Water Park at Cirencester in Gloucestershire was certainly a new species for me, and I was able to spend an hour or more absorbing its taxonomic features. It was here that I met the infamous 'Navigation Man'. I am sure many readers may have met this irritating enigma, as, in one form or another, he appears from the undergrowth at many localities to tell one how inadvisable was the chosen route to get to the site.

'Have you seen it yet?' is his loaded opening gambit and one suspects who he might be. 'Did you come far?' and one's suspicions are fuelled. 'Oh, right. How did you get here?' and one's heart sinks. The reply is irrelevant, as he invariably knows a much better route, one that he always used when he lived in 'your necks of the woods'. Inevitably, his choice is faster, shorter, more direct, less beset by traffic problems and passes fewer speed cameras. He guarantees arriving at the bird long before you every time. He did his best to spoil my Whiskered Tern, but could not, as I had decided to leave anyway. I simply gave him my best Clint Eastwood glare and walked away happy in the knowledge that, on this occasion at least, I had escaped lightly. On driving off, I noticed him approach someone else and felt a pang of sympathy for them.

On the 17th, Nessie and I charged at great speed to the RSPB Nature Reserve at Minsmere, Suffolk, where an Alpine Accentor had been reported. Fortunately, we had very good views of this scarce vagrant, which neither of us had seen before. There were many people present, and I suddenly heard someone answer their mobile phone with the words, 'Oh, hi Lee'. He turned to look directly at me and then answered a very obvious question by saying: 'Yes, he is.' That was the moment I realized with great discomfort that I was being watched. I did not like it but, at the same time, I supposed that at least I was being taken seriously. Just how seriously was yet to be appreciated.

Unfortunately, I was not being watched at my Snettisham and Heacham patch on the 5th. At about 11.30 a.m, I noticed a large raptor drifting in from the south-west. As Marsh Harriers are a common sight here, I assumed at first it was that species. Something seemed different about the way it flew, so I watched it with closer scrutiny. After a few moments, I became convinced that my suspicions were justified, as the wings were held in a flatter 'V' than those of a Marsh Harrier and its wing beats were shallower and less frequent. The large bird approached ever closer, and, as it did so, I was sure I was watching something special. Eventually it circled no more than 50 feet above my head, dragging behind it a conspicuously concave tail. It was a Black Kite! It sailed off into the distant south, as I strained my eyes to grasp on to its image for as long as possible. The excitement was such that all I could do was sit in the fragrant grass and bathe in the memory of what I had just seen. As usual, on my return to *The Enterprise*, I reported my day's findings to RBA. On hearing my account, I was advised not to make public my 'claim' of the Black Kite as their identification is always so contentious: most turn out to be Marsh Harriers or Red Kites. On getting home, I was given the same advice by Ian Burrows. This at once disappointed me and dissipated the thrill I had experienced, but my friends' logic was inescapable. 'Norfolk. BLACK KITE just south of Heacham' therefore did not appear on the pager that day. If only someone else had been there, someone, that is, other than Lee or John.

Nightingales sang on Salthouse Heath as each dusk enveloped the tired days and the first Swift arrived hurriedly in Sculthorpe on the 29th. My total was 277. Most was well in my birding world, but an empire of white-clad footballers was crumbling in Yorkshire. Leeds United was coming apart at the seams.

May – The Lochans of Mercury

May is a month that I look forward to every year with great excitement, for it heralds my second annual visit to the country I love – Scotland. When I first went birding there some twelve years ago, it would take a fortnight to find all that I wanted to see and, even then, I would occasionally fail. These days, with experience and better planning, I can see all the Scottish specialities in just over a week. It's a bitter-sweet pill, as I would prefer to have an excuse to stay there longer and simply enjoy the place with its cocktail of ruggedness and hospitality. In recent years I have included a trip to the Outer Hebrides and I can now no longer imagine, or even bear the thought of, a spring without The Uists and Benbecula – such is the magic of those timeless islands. Each year I dream of visiting St Kilda. I have read in wonderment so much about its people. As I set off this year I would again harbour such dreams but, as usual, I would just as happily settle for the peace of the Caledonian pinewoods and the awe of the Highlands. Given time, I hoped to visit my spiritual 'home from home' at Loch Ness where the rarest of all rare animals will one day surely greet me with a pleading prehistoric glance before sliding into watery oblivion. I fear, however, that it has probably now gone the way of the Great Auk – driven to extinction by the pressures of the modern world. If there really is a place where Plesiosaurs live out their days, then it is here at Loch Ness and every year I watch in the hope of seeing this most elusive of creatures. However, I would have to wait a little while for this year's pilgrimage.

Much closer to home, Norfolk was by now producing its expected scarcer migrants in the form of Temminck's Stint and Curlew Sandpiper at Cley and Montagu's Harrier, again at Cley and also at Holme where they use the inland ridge as an aid to their migration. Holme also played host to an elusive Purple Heron, which showed only briefly as it flew clumsily from one side of a ditch to the other. So fleeting was its flight that several people in the 'gallery' missed it altogether. I know that Lee went to see the bird, as a panic-stricken phone call asked me for the best point of access, but I doubt very much that he in fact saw it. A Bluethroat visited Thornham Point, yet again only frustrating views were obtained as the nervous little bird darted for cover at the merest disturbance. I did not even get to see its throat and could not say for sure whether it was white- or red-spotted. I had better luck with a Red-necked Phalarope at Stiffkey Fen. The bird was in summer plumage and was a delight to behold as it pirouetted in the shallow water in search of food with which to fuel its long flight north. I imagined fancifully that I might, in about a week's time, see this very bird again in North Uist.

Lakenheath Fen, which lies on the border between Norfolk and Suffolk, became alive with the songs of warblers counterpointed with that of a visiting Nightingale. Dawn there was a warm bathtub of soothing melodies. The patchwork of poplar plantations along the river Little Ouse is home to the area's most spectacular songster – the Golden Oriole. As I approach a favoured stand, the lilting notes that float on the heavy morning air always remind me of the sounds one might hear in a tropical rainforest. Despite their startling plumage, they are surprisingly difficult to see and one often leaves without a view. However, the song alone is worth the visit. The rest of the Fen is usually rewarding at this time of the year and often harbours Black Tern, Garganey, Hobby and many waders. On the 17th, I saw no fewer than 13 Common Sandpipers there and for several days a pair of Black-winged Stilts was present. Unfortunately, I did not see the latter.

The shingle ridge that runs from Cley to Blakeney Point is not for the faint-hearted, as the eight miles round walk is exhausting. The stones sap one's strength with every step. One feels as if one is walking through them rather than on them. A northerly element to the wind, and perhaps rain, which is essential for finding rare birds there, does nothing for its hospitality. Even so, if the weather conditions look promising during spring and autumn, it is worth the effort, as there is every possibility of turning up a 'goodie' or two. (No, I have never seen Bill Oddie there).

On the 3rd, Ian and I decided to try our luck and, armed with lots of coffee, water and 'butties', off we trudged. As is often the case, there were plenty of common migrants such as Wheatear, Chiffchaff, Winchat and Whimbrel. On the sea we found three dawdling Red-breasted Mergansers and a fierce-looking Great Skua. Near the 'half-way house', our considerable efforts were rewarded by finding an unusual chiffchaff skulking in the wet *Sueda*. Several times we saw the grey bird as, again and again, we pursued it through the dense plants. Finally we heard it call and the plaintive descending '*tsuwee*' confirmed its identity as Siberian Chiffchaff. The most remarkable event of the day, though, was an extraordinary movement of hirundines. There seemed to be a continuous westerly flight of Sand Martins, House Martins and, particularly, Swallows. This migration peaked between 11.30 a.m. and 2.30 p.m. During those three hours, we estimated about a thousand Swallows passed by. Amongst them were several of the form *transivita,* which is a seductive rufous colour on the underparts where our common form is white. I had never seen it before and so was delighted. The beauty of a day like that is the sheer joy of birding and recording a natural spectacle. I remember wondering what Lee was up to whilst I was being productive.

On the 7th, Ian and I did something else productive. The Norfolk Ornithologists' Association (NOA) held an annual sponsored 24-hour bird race. We decided to enter the event, which, in 2002, was intended to raise money for rebuilding the steps to the Association's reserve visitor centre at Walsey Hills, near Cley. Those old steps were perilous, and we all feared for the safety of Tom Fletcher, the warden, who had to negotiate them every day. With a good cause in mind and the prospect of a few year ticks to be gained, I planned our campaign like a military exercise and away we went. As it happened, I did not get any additions to my list, but we did see 135 bird species and collected well over £400 in sponsorship funds. The highlight was undoubtedly watching a gigantic female Goshawk losing its temper with a Red-tailed Hawk, that old friend from Thetford Forest. Again I wondered what Lee was doing that day since nothing important came up on our pagers.

On the afternoon of the 26th I was at home with Nessie having a wonderful roast chicken dinner. It was to be my last decent meal for some time because I was about to leave for Scotland where, doubtless, I would be eating canned food for many days. Halfway through my 'Last Supper', the pager announced the presence of a Black Stork near Stibbard, some ten minutes drive from my home. There was nothing for it – I had tried and failed several times to see this bird, and it would possibly be my last opportunity, as I doubted it would wait for my return from Scotland. With as many apologies as I could invent, I sped away. Fortunately, I saw the bird quite well and returned home to the cold remains of my dinner and a surprisingly forgiving wife. This bolstered my confidence for the forthcoming trip, and I drove north in the sure and certain knowledge of sweet success. My only regret was leaving Nessie behind, but perhaps I would find another of the same name in the Great Glen.

Being away from southern England at this time of the year was a risky business – a fact made all too clear by dipping the Lesser Grey Shrike at Dawlish Warren, Devon. I therefore needed to make my northern venture as efficient as possible so that I could get home quickly. The shrike was just one of those things and, although missing it annoyed me, nothing else could be done and there were still many Scottish species to see. At this point, John was ahead in the Surfbird table but had already 'done' Scotland. All being well, my return would see me again back in the lead. Lee had now become reticent regarding his tally, and from here on I never really knew what his total was. I was becoming suspicious of his spurious reasons for failing to declare his current total. There was little I could do about it and decided to ignore the problem for the time being and concentrate on my own efforts.

Scotland is a very different world to Norfolk (and Hertfordshire, come to that) and whenever I start the long drive, I always mentally, and sometimes verbally, point my finger in a northerly direction and say: 'Engage!' Even so, 'Warp Ten' could not get me there fast enough and unfortunately my *Enterprise* was considerably slower than Captain Picard's. Consequently, I have learned to be patient to a degree. One way which helps is to make sure that launch time is such that ETA is at dawn – thus allowing a full day's birding. Darkness is usually a waste of time anyway so I spend it travelling. Another is to have 'punctuation' markers along the way. Once the Lake District is reached one is almost out of England. The Scottish border means that dear 'Old Blighty' is in the rear-view mirror. One realizes then just how big Scotland is. It is still a considerable distance to Glasgow and yet, for the birder, one is still not really even then in Scotland. Still, it is a landmark nonetheless. I start to get excited when, eventually, I see signs for Inverness for I know that in a couple of hours time I may be having breakfast in those magical Speyside forests, where a male Capercaillie would be eying my fry-up – and me too – with aggressive intent. This time, though, I would push on to the Kyle of Lochalsh where the extortionately expensive toll bridge would carry me to the picturesque island of Skye. The southern half of Skye is mountainous and foreboding and, in my experience, some of the people there drive like maniacs. Even someone in a hurry, such as myself on this occasion, cannot fail to be struck by the sheer awe of the place but, inexplicably, it is still treated like a racetrack. Once Portree is passed, life changes for the better. The mountains largely give way to a more benign landscape and calmness pervades. Nevertheless, although hundreds of miles from home, I am still hours from my destination and impatience nags at that calmness like toothache. Another landmark though, and another punctuation mark in the paragraph of the trek.

The next point of reference is the port of Uig. I have many memories of Uig. It was here that Nessie and I stayed on our very first Scottish holiday and it was here where we got happily drunk in the quayside pub and watched a small flock of Twites, playing around a child's swing and slide. It was here also where I listened on the radio just a year ago, as Leeds United got summarily kicked out of the European Champions League semi-final – the beginning of one empire's decline. For the first time I mused on the prospects of me being instrumental in the temporary crumbling of another.

Still the journey dragged on. It seems that the nearer one is to one's goal, the further away it is. I was now just a couple of hours from Lochmaddy, in North Uist, but if *The Enterprise* seemed slow, the ferry across was ponderous by comparison. Every cloud has a silver lining, as many comical Puffins and several stately Manx Shearwaters accompanied the crossing. The occasional skuas that passed included two Long-tailed Skuas and no less than 35 Pomarine Skuas, the latter as a few discrete flocks. The Great Skuas still seemed angry – despite having left Norfolk. I hoped to see a European Storm-petrel and perhaps even a Leach's Storm-petrel, but both were elsewhere. A few clumsy Black Guillemots paddled on scarlet feet through the crystal clear waters at our bows. Finally, I arrived in the Outer Hebrides. As I steered *The Enterprise* on to *terra firma* once more I felt, I must admit, important.

Within minutes of my arrival, I was astonished at the sight of a displaying Short-eared Owl. At one moment it clapped its wings above its body and the next it rolled them almost into a tube below. In Norfolk, I had seen many Short-eared Owls but never like this. I was reminded of comments made to me on many occasions about the beauty of seeing birds in their natural environment rather than as storm-assisted lost souls. How right those assessments are. I am usually content to sleep in *The Enterprise*, but this trip was already, and was to be, particularly taxing, so I decided to stay at a small bungalow I knew where Nessie and I had lodged on our previous visit. Happily it was next to a pub. I not only fancied a couple of pints but felt that I had earned them, and one never knows whom one might meet over a 'wee dram'. After all, I was so close to St Kilda, and many of the islanders must surely have a boat. The lady who runs the B&B actually remembered Nessie and me staying before and welcomed me as if I were a long-lost relative. After cutting a deal for just a bed for the night and listening to her tales of how some take advantage of such an arrangement by using primus stoves in their rooms to cook meals, I floated on an air of contentment to the pub. A young couple were there who appeared to be in lust and I wondered what the future held for her apart from motherhood and, him aside, unemployment. I hoped that love would be in the equation somewhere, but doubted its value to them when convenience seemed more realistic. Several middle-aged men came in, bought small bottles of spirits and left. No one stayed long, and my hope of finding a friendly skipper evaporated like warm brandy. The young couple played a meaningless game of pool, which the girl dutifully lost, and they too drifted silently out towards the mocking sounds of the Corncrakes. I never saw them again. On returning to my digs, I opened the window of my bedroom. Those same birds sang a sensuous song to one who already loved them. I fell into a deep and dreamless sleep.

On the following day I found many Corncrakes hiding in the emergent irises and was lucky enough to see some of them. Three Red-necked Phalaropes graced Loch Fada, and I was, as usual, delighted to see native Rock Doves in several localities. These ancestors of the Trafalgar Square multitudes are now restricted to the far north of our islands, and many birders will never have had the opportunity to see one. I recommend they make the effort. At Loch Druidibeg I watched a pair of Golden Eagles and had the pleasure of showing them to a couple of visitors who had never seen this magnificent species before. Hooded Crows in their grey waistcoats were crisp and plentiful. Several Great Northern Divers, some in almost full summer plumage, floated offshore and a Common Snipe unwittingly introduced me to her chick at Caenn a Gharaidh. At this last place, I saw a Sabine's Gull flying purposefully north-west. Although I knew the bird was present in the area, I was still very pleasantly surprised to find it. After locating all my target species, I determined to simply enjoy the islands and the abundance of birds. On the morrow I had to leave. Dozens of Redshanks and Lapwings scolded the unwary with frantic squeals from every field, and the hebridean Starlings, which nest noisily in the dry stonewalls, were abundant and beautifully marked. During the latter half of the eighteenth and the early part of the nineteenth centuries, this species suffered a severe decline in Scotland and almost became extinct on the mainland. Thankfully, it survived in the Outer Hebrides and its genetic isolation there has doubtlessly played a part in producing a form which some authorities believe to be subspecific. At certain points along the coast, notably at Aird an Runair, Corn Buntings rattle their bunches of car keys like a yuppie with a new Ferrari. Even statelier than an Italian sports car are the Hen Harriers that glide over the desolate landscape. During severe westerly winds, sea-watching can be phenomenal with thousands of shearwaters passing offshore at Aird an Runair and Griminish. Nearly all will be Manx Shearwaters, but Sooty Shearwaters are sometimes seen. Skuas are common too in such conditions, and it is quite reasonable to expect all four species, though the Long-tailed Skua is usually scarce. Having said that, Nessie and I once saw two fly low over the car at Aird an Runair car park.

One should always stop and examine gull flocks as one can sometimes be rewarded with jewels in the form of dainty Iceland and brutish Glaucous Gulls. Real rarities occur from time to time, and it was in these islands that I saw my first Greater Yellowlegs. Snowy Owls visit occasionally, yet I have never been fortunate enough for our journeys to coincide. Competitive twitching necessitates haste, but it would be a crime to visit these islands and not take time to simply sit and enjoy them. I challenge anyone who is prepared to listen to do just that and then tell me if I am wrong.

The wonder of birding in such a place is exhausting, and, at the end of each day, a few quiet drinks and an early night are all that I desire. Serenading Corncrakes accompanied the short walk to the pub, and the final evening was, as ever, tinged with sadness, as I bid them farewell for another year. On entering the bar for the last time that year, I found two young men in football kits playing pool and drinking lager after a training session. I spoke only briefly to them, as they did not seem to like the look of me, but they sounded knowledgeable about their sport. One was a Chelsea supporter, although had never been to Stamford Bridge or, it seems, further south than Glasgow. Both smiled ruefully when they discovered I was a Leeds fan, and we reminisced about the club's former Scottish stars, such as Billy Bremner and Peter Lorimer. For a short while I thought we might be friends, but their natural wariness of strangers soon became the dominant instinct. The landlord was less reticent that evening, and we talked of the islands, the social and economic problems therein and how the local constabulary occupied themselves in a place where crime is practically

Chapter 5

unknown. I learned that their main concern was with drink-driving – a sin that appeared to me to inspire street credibility amongst the young and ambivalence with their elders. I left the topic of conversation a wiser man too, as I also found out that a zealous policeman is well within his rights to 'nick' you for sleeping in your car when over the limit, no matter what your intentions. I have since had this confirmed by a friend who is an ex-copper; so beware of that warming nightcap – unless, of course, you are looking for a nice warm cell for the night! As we spoke, the subject of St Kilda arose, and I was excited to discover that a regular drinker in the pub, a pilot, visited the island often and, with appropriate persuasion, would probably take me there. Unfortunately, he would not be around for a few days, and so my dream was gone for another year. Disconsolately I trudged back to my digs, wishing that I were not in such a hurry to leave. So deep were my thoughts that I do not remember hearing the Corncrakes but at least mentally I had already said 'bye-bye'.

The following morning was made in Heaven. I drove to Griminis Head where a Red-breasted Flycatcher had been seen. The light was electric, and not a breath of wind stirred to alternate its current. I docked *The Enterprise* at the side of the road and gazed in wonderment over the small lochans at the side of the road. In the silver unruffled air they nuzzled between the breasts of moorland vegetation like pools of mercury, heavy with early morning sleep. When life seems cruel, I merely have to close my eyes and revisit that morning. What a lucky man I am. I wondered if Lee is so lucky. I doubted it as I do not think he would have noticed those Lochans of Mercury.

Little was happening during the ferry crossing back to Uig. This gave me the chance to finalize my thoughts about the next phase of my tour. The White-billed Diver is a very scarce bird indeed around British waters, but one has to consider the immensity of the Scottish coastline where the paucity of recorders and the birds are mainly found. Although I was on a

May – The Lochans of Mercury

twitching 'mission', the scientist in me could not ignore the opportunity to do a little research. I had identified 26 sites on the north-west coast which I believed may harbour this species and set out convinced that it was more common than anyone suspected. With this in mind, I set course for Cape Wrath. At Ullapool, I bought something that I was assured was a beef burger, and a kindly American gentleman pointed out that my front offside tyre was flat. Dishevelled, I admitted to him that the steering had '...seemed a bit funny...', thanked him with a handshake during which my knuckles cracked painfully and drove away clutching my greasy purchase. In my mirror, I could see the American shaking his head in disbelief. 'What strange folk those English are,' he presumably thought. I changed the offending wheel and threw the burger away. Some gulls ate the bread.

My next birding port of call was Durness where, at Sango Bay, there had been a previous report of a White-billed Diver. As if by magic there he was, cocking a snook with his upturned bill at his 'lesser' congeners in the form of Great Northern and Red-throated Divers. Gannets, skuas and auks in their hundreds looked on as I congratulated myself at being so clever as to find that imperious bird. Fortunate I may have been but clever, it seems, I was not as I searched the remaining 25 sites without success. All day it took, too, but at least I could hope to pick up one of those gigantic White-tailed Eagles along the way at Gruinard Bay. Many readers will know the lay-by on the A832 from which one can look out over Gruinard Island where Anthrax may still be present. From here, if one is patient, White-tailed Eagles are almost sure to show, and amazing views of those huge 'flying doors' can sometimes be had. On this particular visit, the weather was truly awful, and I had to employ my stove inside the car in order to heat the indescribably bad canned 'delectation' that was to serve as dinner. Having done so, and feeling strangely sated, I turned my attention outwards. I had

Chapter 5

already scanned the island with my binoculars and found nothing. Several people had since gathered and were now doing the same. Imagine their surprise when a lone voice shouted at the skies, 'White-tailed eagle!' whilst all others were peering forlornly at the deserted rock. As the massive bird glided over the road, cameras clicked and whirred and many an expletive was uttered. The nicest word I heard through my growing homesickness was 'Thanks'. The saddest thought I had was that the magnificent creature meant nothing to me but a tick. I put it down to fatigue and drove south.

I know of a site where Temminck's Stints breed and I called by to see if they were at home. Often this species does not arrive on its nesting grounds until early June, and I feared I might be a little early. My fears were justified, but the delay gave me a little more time in which an apparently absent Snowy Egret might show. A Broad-billed Sandpiper was now in Devon so I was informed, and I thought – insanely – that it may be a good idea to head straight down there. However, a conversation with Andrew at RBA changed my mind. I was pessimistic about seeing the egret, but his 'gut feeling' told him the bird was still around. His enthusiasm caught on, so I decided to stay at Carrbridge and see what the pager said next morning. Almost unbelievably it informed me the bird had been seen the previous day at Castleton Bay, near Lochgilphead. A long detour and much searching found the site, and there I gratefully re-acquainted myself with that lovely White Heron. I left the bird on the last day of May. On that same day, the Broad-billed Sandpiper had departed but a Common Rosefinch was singing at Weybourne in Norfolk. I made it there by 8.40 p.m. and saw the bird through exhausted eyes which I then closed in the welcoming arms of my wife. They remained closed for fourteen hours.

Throughout the month, a steady trickle of twitches kept the odometer busy. The longest distance travelled was to the Isles of

Scilly where a Lesser Kestrel hung defiantly on mighty winds, and I was fortunate enough to get a cancelled seat on the otherwise fully-booked helicopter from Penzance to see it. This bird is a rare species indeed, but I have to be honest and admit that I was not particularly impressed since it is extremely similar to our own Common Kestrel. Consequently, I did not tolerate the appalling weather for long. At Marazion that day, I and a young couple who were just beginning their birding adventure together, watched a gale-battered Citrine Wagtail that was never seen again and three Pomarine Skuas close inshore, the latter magnificent with their exotic spoon-shaped tails.

A journey to Yorkshire provided the best views of White-winged Black Tern I have ever had, and an elusive Thrush Nightingale sang briefly at Spurn Point. I think I saw the bird for a fleeting second but could not be sure. It did not matter though, as Lee had said at Gibraltar Point, Lincolnshire, the previous year that to hear the song alone counts as a year tick. It was in the notebook. The longest 'stake-out' was for a Great Reed Warbler at Frensham Little Pond, Surrey, where I waited for nearly four hours to hear the bird's colossal song and gaze upon its sleek form. The prettiest star was the Lesser Sand Plover at Rimac National Nature Reserve in Lincolnshire. With its delightful pastel plumage, it reminded me of a lovely girl who craves attention and feigns disinterest. I fell in love with 'her' within seconds but I don't think 'she' noticed. To my astonishment, despite this being only the third record of the species in Britain, Lee later told me that he did not go to see it. To this day, I remain mystified by that decision.

The prize for the 'dirtiest tick' was certainly the Least Sandpiper at Drayton Basset in Staffordshire. Never have I seen such appalling liquid mud. I was literally covered from toe to knee in grime. This, coupled with the then ever-growing prospect of being thrown off the site before seeing the bird, made for a miserable day indeed. 'Go on, mate, have a heart; I've

The Author in north Norfolk, April 1991, willing to consider any new 'tick' at this early stage in his birding career. Photo by Debbie Wood

Scientific times at Rothamsted, July 2001. Nicotine and caffeine close to hand. Photo by Phil Gould

Black-eared Wheatear
All photos by Gary Thoburn

Woodchat Shrike

Grasshopper Warbler

White Stork

Silver-studded Blue
All photos by the author

Norfolk Hawker. Strumpshaw Fen, Norfolk.
Britain's rarest dragonfly

White Admiral

Isles of Scilly Meadow Brown

Purple Heron
All photos by Gary Thoburn

White-billed Diver

White-winged Black Tern

Common Rosefinch

Glen Gour, Inverness-shire. Home of the Golden Eagle and Scottish Dark Green Fritillary. Photo by the author

Watching the Stilt Sandpiper, Pennington Marshes, Hampshire, July 2002. Photo by Phil Gould

Chapter 5

driven all the way from Fakenham!' seemed to do the trick. The security man did have a heart and he wished me well in my search, though he warned me to be quick about it.

I mentioned earlier that Lee phoned me regarding the Purple Heron at Holme. The date was the 22nd of May, and that day proved to be another turning point in the year. During the conversation we discussed John Pegden's indignation at being unable to hold the lead against me. Lee told me, with all the arrogance he could muster, that he knew where I was all the time and was aware of all the birds I was seeing. I was at the same time both flattered and disturbed by his statement. That he should take me so seriously was surely a compliment, yet I objected to my progress being monitored so closely, and this short conversation was to change my attitude to birding, and particularly towards Lee, forever. My total was on 308, and it was now becoming obsessively the most important thing in my life.

June and July – the half-time break

It seemed strange that, with the game in full flow, a lull in the form of July was soon to arrive. However, June is the month when one can consolidate by gathering up any missing summer migrants, and rarities are still on the cards. By now the Swifts had moved into Sculthorpe in force. Up and down The Street they chased each other like flocks of screeching Banshees, cursing their rivals' perceived aerial dexterity. How I love these birds, and how evocative they are of an English summer.

On the radio, Henry Blofeld guiding us impishly through the last few overs of the day; on the village green the crack of willow on leather and the hopeful call of '*Owzaat*' as the blacksmith dismantles the butcher's wicket; foaming ale from a pewter pot in the pavilion with the vicar and the aromatic smoke from the gamekeeper's pipe; the parish church clock announcing the end of play and the sight and sound of swifts chasing insects through the scent of freshly cut grass on a warm evening breeze. These are a few of my favourite things about being a rural Englishman. Others can be found in the place I have chosen to live. Quails are by now singing their strange song '*Wet me lips, wet me lips*' from the fields around Choseley, where they are accompanied at dawn by rattling Corn Buntings. At night, the chirring Nightjars gave Nessie and me a magical evening on Salthouse Heath where their curiosity over my flapping white handkerchief brought them to within inches of our ducking heads. Nightingales serenaded our antics. The occasional hopeful Hobby hawked the Swifts that nest beneath the pan tiles of our roof, and larger raptors, Common Buzzard and Honey Buzzard, the latter a scarce breeding bird, soared on thermals over Great Ryburgh.

Chapter 6

As one might expect, a few rarities strayed into Norfolk, including a singing Icterine Warbler at RSPB Titchwell on the 6th of June. I, like many before me, had not heard the song of this species before, as it usually arrives in Britain during autumn when their need for vocalization has passed. It is rich, melodic and as full of masterly mimicry as that of a Marsh Warbler. I was fortunate to be able to compare the two, since a Marsh Warbler had been singing at Weybourne only three days previously and its qualities were still fresh in my mind. I wondered with sadness if that bird had been displaced from its breeding site in Kent where I used to visit them annually but which had recently suffered at the hands of egg thieves. What punishment would be appropriate for one guilty of such a crime, I wondered? Titchwell also played host to a Surf Scoter and, just as I had considered whether I would meet the Red-necked Phalarope at Stiffkey in Scotland, I liked to think that I was watching one of the very birds that were in my telescope at Largo Bay a few months previously. A nice fantasy but little more, I suspect.

Fantasy may well be the best word to describe the credentials of the White-headed Duck at Hardley Flood in Norfolk, although those 'in the know' seemed to like it. That was good enough for me. I liked it too, with its broken Roman nose and its scruffy plumage, it reminded me of a noble but less than skilful boxer. Ian Burrows kept telling me that a Pectoral Sandpiper was sure to arrive in Norfolk sooner or later. I did not share his confidence and was ever prepared to travel a great distance to find one. However, he was right; the only problem was that it was within the grounds of Pensthorpe Wildfowl Park, near my home, where a very expensive entry fee precluded many (by choice) from seeing the bird. We went anyway and a guest of ours paid for us. I saw only one other Pectoral Sandpiper that year, and it was a long way from Norfolk.

My phone rang. It was Lee. Apparently the Canvasback Duck at Pennington Flash, in Manchester, was 'a load of rubbish'. During the conversation I remembered a previous discussion regarding a Hooded Merganser in Northumberland. This bird was also 'rubbish' and could not possibly be a genuine vagrant. It must surely have escaped from a wildfowl collection and was certainly not worth the long journey. At the time, I did not realize that Lee had already seen the bird and I was later astonished to hear his imperious edict that it was, in his opinion, 'acceptable'. These words of wisdom came the day after the bird left – never to be seen again. As we talked about the Canvasback, slight feelings of betrayal came seeping through my defences, and I resolved to go and see the 'dodgy' duck. I felt that I was being taken for a fool and I had had enough. Like a featherweight in the ring against Lennox Lewis, I threw my first pathetic punch and made out that I would not go to Manchester. One small pat it may have been, but, like any good boxer, I was feeling my way against an opponent whose competitiveness I did not know nor fully appreciate. Confusion, for the time being, was my best ally against an opponent who seemed far more ring-wise than me. It seems to me that ducks are the easiest way to either gain or dismiss records, depending on one's requirements at the time. Was the Falcated Duck at Minsmere in Suffolk (which I was 'allowed' to count) any more viable than the Hooded Merganser? Was the Canvasback phonier than the Bufflehead at Great Livermere in Suffolk? Ultimately, no one can really know where these ducks have come from and I wonder now whether, for the purpose of year-listing, some blanket rule should be made. It is my belief that these birds are available to everyone and, apart from *known* escapes, are worth a 'gander' anyway. Such visits are often made for 'insurance purposes' in case the bird is accepted as being a genuine vagrant at a later date. It would save many an argument if they were all countable as year ticks and inclusion on life-lists was (as is already the case) deferred until the British Birds Rarity Committee made their decision. It is appropriate to use the word 'committee' here, as no one person, no matter what

Chapter 6

he or she may consider themselves to be, should have the sole authority to sit in judgement on such issues – more especially if they have a vested interest in the outcome of the decision made.

My phone rang again. The name 'Lee' came up on the display. Until now I had enjoyed seeing this but by the end of June I rarely looked forward to the ensuing conversation. It was the 30th, I was at Cresswell Ponds in Northumberland and I had just reported the White-rumped Sandpiper to RBA.

'What's this about a White-rumped Sand?' an incredulous voice asked.

'I'm looking at it as we speak,' was my reply.

'Who drove up with you?' was the next question.

On telling him that I had travelled alone, there was a stunned silence that seemed to last for hours followed by the observations that I was 'crazy' to drive all that way for such a bird and that I had 'lost the plot'. Evidently, Lee did not consider this species sufficiently rare to make an eight hour round journey. Or was he simply annoyed that he was in Perthshire at the time and was therefore unlikely to see it? We ended the conversation on good terms; I ended the day with a White-rumped Sandpiper and the bird ended its day elsewhere and had gone by the time Lee arrived at Cresswell.

There is little doubt that another White-rumped Sandpiper would probably arrive in Britain, yet no one can say when, where or indeed if. The Cresswell bird was available and it had to be 'got'. As it happened, another one did turn up, only a short way from Fakenham. However, I was in Harpenden at the time and, for reasons I shall leave to the reader's imagination, it was probably better that I did not drive. I found this situation highly amusing as the mission was already accomplished although my thirst was not yet sated. Later in the year I found it even more amusing, as a regular visitor to Titchwell, to see a third White-rumped Sandpiper there which remained for several weeks. But I never regretted that visit to Northumberland or the comments that it caused – the most significant one being, in hushed tones, 'I think you're trying to beat me.'

By now, long journeys were becoming routine. I tried as much as possible not to be away overnight as I did not think it fair on the ever-patient Nessie. This led to a familiar routine whereby I would leave home during the small hours and drive through the night in the hope of being home for teatime – or opening time – according to the stress of the journey and its success.

Some of these trips were straightforward and enjoyable. I particularly recall the trip to see a Savi's Warbler at Dungeness, Kent. The dawn welcomed me with warming arms, as I sat overlooking a small pond listening to the bush cricket-like song of my quarry. Every now and then, he would appear atop a reed stem and buzz with all his heart, his thick rounded tail balancing his tiny weight and his white throat trembling through his efforts to call in a mate or deter a rival. There was a great hatch of aquatic flies that morning. As they emerged from the ponds in their tens of thousands they landed on the nearest object they could find and dragged themselves from the remains of their pupal skins, leaving the ghost of their former selves behind. For many of them, I was the closest convenient landing post and I went home covered in their white discarded cases. Had I been a trout fisherman, I think I could have fed well at breakfast.

My trip with Phil to Pennington Marshes, Hampshire, was another that I remember fondly for I love the place anyway, and my memories of it draw me there again and again. To go there and see a Stilt Sandpiper on a perfect sunny day in good company was a joy. This species is not only a major rarity but, in my view, one of the most beautifully marked of all the waders. Of its summer plumage, it retained much of the barring on the breast and shades of rufous below the supercilium. Its long legs added to the overall grace of the bird. We had plenty of time to spare and, although we saw few other birds of note, were grateful to soak up the atmosphere and return home contented.

In hindsight, the funniest trip perhaps was to visit the bee-eaters at Bishop Middleham in County Durham. Ian and I decided that, bee-eaters being bee-eaters, one has little chance of success on a long-distance twitch since no sooner do they arrive than they almost inevitably move quickly on their way. My attitude towards the game had changed considerably since the far off days of the winter and, despite advice to the contrary, off I went. North along the A1 I sped until level with Leeds when the unthinkable happened. – 'Co. Durham. No sign of European Bee-eaters at Bishop Middleham Quarry,' said the pager. 'Bloody idiot,' I said to myself for undertaking such a stupid task. I was fed up and underfed so decided to call at a garage for a sulk and a sandwich. There I phoned Nessie and told her of the development. In her usual way she expressed disappointment at my attitude and assured me that they would be back. How do women know these things when all logic dictates they must be wrong? Within minutes, the birds were reported as still being present. I did not need the 'I told you so' when I phoned home again but I got it anyway and did a fair impression of *The Dukes of Hazard* as I left the garage forecourt. As many of you may know, the bee-eaters not only remained long enough for me to see them on the 3rd of June but also for some 15,000 other birders between then and September, by which time they had fledged two young. It's a funny old game. I learned an important lesson here. Never simply turn around and go home at the first sign of negative news. Pull over, have a cup of coffee and a bite to eat – even take a nap for a while. Most importantly, wait and see what happens.

Often a trip does not work out quite the way one plans it. On the 8th of June, I set off for Barrow-in-Furness, in Lancashire, near where a Squacco Heron had been reported. I have no idea how long the drive took, but my notebook shows that I saw the bird at 10.20 in the morning, which would probably make it about seven hours or so. Should anyone in their right mind consider driving for fourteen hours to spend fifteen minutes with an ugly bird? That my sanity was now in doubt was obvious to all who knew me, and by the halfway point of the return journey I was asking some serious questions myself. Worse was to come in the form of a pager message reporting a Marsh Sandpiper near Leeds. On reaching the junction of the M6 and M1, a rational person would have got onto the A14 and headed east towards home. Instead, I turned *The Enterprise* north onto the M1 in the direction of Leeds. It was not until well after 5.00 p.m. that I finally decided that I needed to see the inside of a pint glass, and perhaps a counsellor, and set off south. I saw the bird though, and met several bewildered, but defiant, Leeds United supporters in the process.

I was not popular when I arrived home and was reminded of an episode of *Rab C. Nesbit* wherein the hero popped out to get some sausages for his long-suffering wife. He returned several days later after a fierce drinking session with his mates. 'I got the sausages, Mary Doll,' was his opening gambit. 'I got the birds, Ness Monster,' was mine. Neither was successful. Perhaps I should have gone home *before* going to the pub. I'll know better next time. At least the trip was a success, unlike the one to Derwent Water in Co. Durham on the 20th of June.

The Spotted Sandpiper I saw there was an absolute delight as it displayed and sang in his spotty summer livery. It was the Collared Flycatcher that bothered me though, as it was hours away near Pagham, Sussex. Add to that a reported 'Orange-billed Tern' in Norfolk and one can imagine the language that filled *The Enterprise*. Fleeing south as fast as I could was in vain, as both birds disappeared before I was even close enough to decide which one to go for. As I left Derwent I saw Lee heading towards the reservoir and it was not long before we were talking on the phone about the best course of action. There simply wasn't one, and we both went home very disappointed indeed. As you may have gathered, I was beginning to feel the strain of my relationship with him, but such circumstances tended to ease the tension somewhat. I admit that I would have been even more upset had Lee seen either of the dipped birds but I could now understand just how galling such missed opportunities can be. I felt sorry for myself, but also for him.

Our ailing friendship was restored to almost good health by my visit to Horseshoe Point in Lincolnshire, on the 18th of July, where a frightened Pacific Golden Plover dodged the many angry warplanes that roared over the marshes. Richard Bromilow and I had been watching White Admiral and Silver-studded Blue butterflies (as well as many dragonflies whose names we did not know) in east Norfolk when we decided to 'go' for the plover. On arrival, the bird had disappeared and could not be relocated. Every time a jet went over, swarms of birds took to the skies and were scattered to the four winds. Our plover was amongst them. From some fifty miles distant, Lee phoned to ask how the situation looked, and when I told him, he talked of giving it up as a bad job. I persuaded him to carry on. Several times he called to find the circumstances unchanged, and I again told him to keep to his plan to come. We would find the bird. Find it someone did, and, in its summer plumage, what a spectacular bird it was. Lee was delighted at the news and arrived in good time to see it, despite the idiotic efforts of two selfish photographers to flush it by attempting too close an approach. I have seen this happen before and I can envisage some very nasty consequences of this behaviour if the 'right' person is upset on the 'wrong' day.

The end of July was reached with 328 species seen, myself physically intact and my relationship with Lee altered but still in one piece. I say physically intact, but mentally the strain was beginning to tell on me. On the 6th of June, Ireland played Spain in an important World Cup Football match, and I would have loved to watch them win in a local pub with my regular footie and beer friends. However, a Broad-billed Sandpiper had been found at Saltholme Pool in Cleveland. After trips to Cumbria, Durham and Yorkshire, to say nothing of many local sorties, I was almost burned out, yet the trip to Cleveland had to be made, as there may not have been another of this species available. A small flock of Dunlins flew over as I arrived and amongst them was something different. It may well have been the Broad-billed Sandpiper but, equally, it may not. I was so low on emotional fuel that I found I did not even care about the bird. I phoned Nessie and told her in a broken voice that I had had enough. I simply felt unable to carry on driving myself into the ground. I could not even face the long journey home. I was beaten. I sat with my arms crossed over the steering wheel of *The Enterprise* and wept with sheer unadulterated exhaustion. Ireland lost.

August – unto the breach once more

Nessie was obviously extremely concerned about the state of my health and, not least, about my competence to drive home from Cleveland. So was I. I had always considered myself to be emotionally very strong – especially when it came to a tough challenge. What I had not bargained for with this particular venture was the amount of time over which the stress would last. It now dawned on me that, like the race for the football league title, this was a marathon, not a sprint, and success or failure could hang on the very last game of the season. Earlier in the year, Lee had said that he would not be able to keep up the pace that I was setting. I was discovering to my cost that these were not idle words. Because Lee is so well known in birding circles and commands respect within the twitching fraternity, he rarely has problems procuring travelling companions who are willing to drive. Because I was relatively unknown within this community, I was finding the travelling extremely difficult and, more often than not, I was doing all the driving myself. No wonder then that I was sinking into a quagmire of fatigue. These questions needed urgent attention if I were not to end up bleeding to death in some God-forsaken roadside ditch or worse, killing an innocent road-user. After some welcome words from Nessie and enough cigars to bring on a mild attack of asthma, I drove home from Cleveland gingerly but safely. The next few days were spent in self-examination and discussion with Nessie and my friends over what was to be done.

The first thing that was hammered relentlessly into me by everyone concerned was that I was not to give up. All my friends know that I am the kind of player who responds best to a kick in the backside rather than the kid glove approach. My backside was, metaphorically speaking, black and blue. After a day or two, I had been shouted at, insulted, derided and verbally assaulted to the point where I thought, 'I'll show you bastards'.

Fortunately, birding was slow at the start of August and I could also relax a little. The problem of being the sole driver was never solved. It was suggested that I send out a message through RBA, asking for lifts every now and then, or at least offering lifts so that I would have company on long journeys. Occasionally I had made some solid friends doing this; unfortunately, the opposite was also true. I naturally do not wish to mention names but I had had some bad experiences giving lifts to people I did not know. One particular chap drove me to despair with his tales of how good a birder he was. He told me his life story from beginning to end (an end which nearly became premature that day), warts and all. He gave me concise accounts of the misdemeanours committed by his 'so-called friends' and the lengths to which they would go to avoid him. There was no conversation, no dialogue; he simply moaned and bragged incessantly. He left an ocean of junk food wrappers and an almost tangible fog of body odour in *The Enterprise*. To make matters worse, he was unlucky. We dipped on two important birds, and it didn't bother him in the least. I hoped with all my heart to drop him off near his home as soon as possible; so imagine my chagrin when he discovered the existence of another rare bird in Norfolk and invited himself to keep me company for a further three hours.

Another important reason for not offering lifts is that I did not want Lee to know where I was going. If, as he claimed, he knew where I was all the time, he would have to work for that information. I was not about to offer it on a plate by advertising it on the pager. The solution to the problem became an inner one. So long as I was aware of the difficulties involved in driving such huge distances I could combat them through more sensible behaviour (more food and drink, more frequent breaks, more rest prior to the trip, etc.). My present state of fragility was due mostly to the fact that I was unaware of the dangers of self-neglect and, to be honest, would probably have ignored them anyway. My friends had told me often enough that I was driving myself too hard, but I chose not to listen. Feeling better, tougher and intrinsically yet indefinably different, I eased myself into the 'second half'.

Only four-day trips were made during August and these resulted in three successes and one failure. In a strange way, the failure was probably the biggest success. On the 2nd, my Bedfordshire birding buddy, Alex McLennan (who, incidentally, has done possibly the three least popular jobs on the planet – policeman, bailiff and football referee) and I went to Netherton in Yorkshire, to look for a Marbled Duck whose credentials seemed plausible.

Not quite so plausible were the directions given to us by an elderly local when asked the whereabouts of a certain road which would have led us to the bird. His pink watery eyes told us that he had been drinking for many hours, but had probably not quite finished. Sleep may later have ruined such plans. The colour of his skin also told us that he had been drinking for many years and that he intended doing so for many more (dialysis may later have proved otherwise). His voice told us he had smoked strong cigarettes since boyhood, and death might soon end those fewest of pleasures. As a young man, I suspect, he knew every street and alleyway in his local village, and I felt that he still considered himself an oracle in such matters. Unfortunately, his faculties were now dulled. He rambled his way through excessively complicated instructions that led us completely in the wrong direction and extended our quest by maybe an hour. Much cursing ensued and from someone with Alex's professional background it was considerable, picturesque and succinct.

A gentleman mowing the lawn for his wife in order to earn

'Brownie points' was more helpful, and eventually we walked along an attractive canal towards the flooded pastures where our duck lived. After much searching and even more bad language, Alex, by some miracle to which only he was privy, spotted an inquisitive head protruding from the long grass which bore the correct markings for a Marbled Duck. Neither of us had seen the species before and we were keen to watch it in the open. We waited and waited until eventually it waddled through the grass and onto the nearby water where it appeared in all its glory like a softly spangled Milky Way. By now, about half a dozen people were watching, all delighted with such a rare sight. The mutual backslapping and congratulations ceased as the bird turned to dabble, revealing a red plastic ring on its right leg. Not a word was uttered. Although most must have seen it, none wished to acknowledge its existence.

I shouted, 'The f***ing thing's married; it's wearing a ring,' and everyone trudged off in the way one does when one's football team has just lost in the semi-final of the FA Cup – despondent and silent, save the odd whispered profanity.

To this day I wonder if anyone else there would have owned up to seeing that ring. I tend to doubt it, as they had plenty of time before I did. The bird was never seen again, and had I kept quiet, I would have had another tick which Lee could not have got. However, had I done so, my conscience would not have allowed me to sit here writing this book. Lee rang and seemed amused at my disappointment and pleased that a trip to Yorkshire was now not necessary.

I later had unsatisfactory views of a Franklin's Gull in Oxfordshire and fleeting views of a Terek Sandpiper in flight in Essex. I am indebted to a car load of lads at the latter site for giving me their parking ticket, which had a couple of hours of life left in it – thus giving me free parking for the duration of my stay. So appalling was that place with its myriad 'Kiss me quick' weekenders that I hoped I would not need to buy another ticket.

Chapter 7

I later decided that the reason for only getting flight views of the bird was that it was desperately trying to escape. What a different story, though, was Elmley in Kent on the 11th. It was a beautiful sunny day in a corner of England that I adore and around which I have wandered happily and frequently with one of my mentors, Neil Davies. After perhaps an hour of waiting and many cups of coffee, a wonderful male Pallid Harrier floated across the shimmering marshes to gasps of delight from the many onlookers. Lee had driven from Cornwall to be there but was leaving as I arrived. He seemed genuinely disappointed that I had not seen the bird and later phoned and encouraged me to stick with it. I was grateful for his concern and wished him well with his search for a White-winged Black Tern at Welney in Norfolk. A renewed friendship pierced the ether that day and my growing distrust of the man was halted. As I watched the magnificent raptor, an endless armada of wind-borne willow-herb seeds sailed across the flat land on rippling hot breezes in search of fertile soil. I was sorry to leave them behind but did so reluctantly and in the knowledge that I would one day see them again in the form of a lovely pink flower, or as host to the snake-like caterpillar of an Elephant Hawk-moth.

Ian Burrows and I spent many a happy hour during the month sea-watching at Cley, and our efforts were rewarded handsomely. One morning, two Long-tailed Skuas came close inshore and, on another, three Leach's Petrels skimmed purposefully across the waves. Arctic and Great Skuas were plentiful, as were Manx and Sooty Shearwaters. The occasional Balearic Shearwater caused excitement and a single Black Tern graced us with its presence on the 27th. As usual, several Cory's Shearwaters were reported, but, unsurprisingly, all I could see were Fulmars. The first snooty Red-throated Divers were now beginning to arrive for their winter holiday. Cley Marshes were also productive. Amongst the Dunlins several Curlew Sandpipers and Little Stints were often to be found and, on the 3rd, two

Broad-billed Sandpipers arrived. These prompted a frenetic phone call from Lee who not only wanted to know if the birds were still present, but also who was in the hide at the time. It appears I was not the only one being watched. 'Is Millington there?' he enquired. That Richard Millington's presence met with such a disgruntled tone irritated me somewhat, as he is an ornithologist (note that I use the word 'ornithologist' rather than 'birder') for whom I have the utmost respect. It was another chip knocked out of the foundations of trust I had in Lee as a putative pal. Ian, Alex and I made a point of leaving before Lee arrived, although I was more concerned about conflict amongst others rather than between us. I did not want to be part of any bad feeling. It was then perhaps that I first felt uncomfortable being an acquaintance of Lee's, a man to whom adversarial feelings appeared to be a way of life. What were his motives? What really made him tick? For now I preferred to ignore these questions. After all, we were presently on good terms. A Red-breasted Flycatcher at Wells Woods in Norfolk prompted yet another call.

'What's it doing?'
'How old is it?'
'What sex is it?'

I wondered if these interrogations collectively meant, 'Are you really there?' Yet another brick in the edifice of suspicion!

Opportunities are ever available for finding my own scarce birds in Norfolk and, whenever I was not on 'twitching duty', I was out in hopeful search. August got off to a great start with the discovery of three Wood Sandpipers at Stiffkey Fen – a species which has so far eluded some experienced birders that I know. It is also a species which reminds me again of happy days in Scotland, where I have watched it display during many still dawns over desolate, wet and otherwise silent moorlands. Fittingly, a Wood Warbler – green, gold and white in the strong sun – greeted me one morning at Stiffkey Woods. Although it did not sing, I was once again reminded of magical journeys to

Scotland where, in the stunted woodlands near Loch Insh, their trilling melodies are a joy and bring a smile to the face of any exhausted birder.

Having returned from an unsuccessful early morning stint on the north Norfolk coast on the 23rd, my mind drifted towards the cricket ground at Leeds where the second day of play was about to start in the third test match of England's series against India. At the end of the first day, India were 236 for two. With the excellent Dravid scoring 110, an exciting day's play was in prospect. England were one up in the series and I was very keen to see the first hour or so of play, as our seam bowlers can often use the early moist atmospheric conditions to swing the ball through the dense air to great effect.

On the road between Moreston and Langham, despite my dreaming of the rattle of Indian wickets, my birding brain still ticked over, and I glanced routinely upwards. There on a telephone wire, to my utter astonishment, was a bee-eater. I discovered quickly that the braking system on *The Enterprise* was in excellent working order and, having 'scraped myself off the windscreen', I jumped out to view my most spectacular find ever. Immediately I phoned RBA and then prayed that someone would find me before the bird flew off. If anyone wanted to accuse me of fabricating a record then this would be a perfect opportunity, as it was likely that such a skittish species would be long gone by the time anyone arrived to corroborate the sighting. I need not have worried. Before long, about fifty people were enjoying the bird as it hawked and called at close quarters. One chap arrived as the bee-eater was perched on the wire and shouted in a very urgent and accurate Lee-like voice, 'Where is it in relation to the Blue Tit?' I don't know whether it was the excitement of such a good find, the relief of having it substantiated, his witticism or a combination of all three, but the tears of laughter rolled down my cheeks. Soon the bird took off west and disappeared from view. Knowing the area well, I fancied my chances of relocating it and so began exploring the nearby minor roads. It was indeed my lucky day and I found it quickly, reported it to RBA, and soon another throng of happy birders formed. Later, in The Horse and Groom in Sculthorpe, many celebratory pints were given a decent burial by Ian and me and, consequently, we remembered little of the afternoon's play in the test match. Perhaps it is just as well. India ended the day on a massive 584 for four, Dravid scoring a magnificent 148 and Sachin Tendulkar a mercurial 193 – his highest ever score against England. India went on to win the match comprehensively and the series was drawn one each. The English batsmen must surely have been watching the telephone wires rather than the Indian bowlers, though I heard no reports of bee-eaters from Leeds at that time.

Only one big trip was planned for August – to the Isles of Scilly with Jason. A fistful of 'lifers' was possible for Jason on this venture. When I met him in the early hours of the 13th, he was bleary-eyed yet very excited. Wilson's Storm-petrel was our main target, but we were dreaming of much more in the shape of shearwaters and European Storm-petrel. The almost mythical Fea's Petrel was being ever more frequently seen, and we were going to be in the right place at the right time. To this end, we hoped to make two pelagic trips aboard *The Kingfisher* out of St Mary's. Her very able skipper, Alec Hicks, is a much-respected bird-finder. We were brimming with confidence. With any luck, Bob Flood would also be aboard and his expertise simply demands respect. Lee had expressed an interest in joining us on this trip, but I preferred not to keep my promise to discuss it with him 'nearer the time' as I needed the edge of seeing rarities in his absence. I was not happy about such an ungenerous attitude and, under normal circumstances, would not have considered adopting it. However, these were not 'normal circumstances'. The Hooded Merganser incident had left me with few illusions as to his regard, or lack of it, for the 'Marquis of Queensbury' rules.

We intended arriving by dawn at Marazion Marsh, near Penzance, in the hope of seeing an Aquatic Warbler. At one time, the site would harbour quite a few of this scarce species each year, but in recent times numbers had fallen dramatically. Whether this was a result of a global population decline or the result of site mismanagement is not clear, although I suspect, like most ecological questions, the answer is multi-faceted. The journey to Cornwall was hindered at times by some fairly serious fog problems, yet our arrival at Marazion was still premature enough to allow forty winks and almost as many cups of strong black coffee. Daybreak was cold and miserable and suppressed our earlier feelings of rampaging confidence, though as the dawn unfolded into early morning, so the temperature and our spirits rose. Stationed at the edge of a small pond surrounded by sedges and reeds, we had one false alarm after another as several Sedge Warblers ferreted around the vegetation. A Water Rail mocked us from its muddy lair and two other silent birders scanned a different part of the marsh to our right. Their body language suggested a severe lack of success. A hushed but excited 'Ade!' from over my shoulder spun me in the direction of a crouched Jason and there, close in front of us, was an Aquatic Warbler doing what this species does best – skulking low down in the sedges trying hard to hide. Very like a Sedge Warbler, but pale ginger with more contrasting dark markings, the doubts lingered until it turned in such a way that the pale central crown stripe allayed all our fears of misidentification. We watched it for many minutes before it clambered clumsily away. The other two birders had already departed and missed a wonderful experience – if only the sight of a pair of mud-spattered lunatics hugging in mutual congratulation. Had I been alone, I too would have gone away empty-handed. Thank Heaven for that little Welshman.

The Scillonian was due to sail from Penzance at around 8.15 a.m., but when we arrived on the quayside, we were told that mechanical problems would delay the ferry's sailing and were politely asked, with that unmistakable corporate smile, to return at 12.30 p.m. My response was as polite as I could muster and was accompanied by my equally unmistakable, 'fairly good impression' of Clint Eastwood's slit-eyed glare from beneath fathoms of Hamlet cigar smoke. I assumed the fact that I had not shaved for several days would intensify this embodiment of disapproval, but the nice lady from The Isles of Scilly Steamship Company evidently had never watched Sergio Leone's *The Good, The Bad and The Ugly* and continued to smile. Defeated and disarmed, we scuttled off to find some breakfast with which to pump up our now deflated muscles and egos. Missing the early crossing to St Mary's was a serious blow to our plans, for we had hoped to see many sea birds on the journey. Morning is generally regarded as the best time for such pursuits. As a compromise, we found a sheltered spot on the edge of the harbour where I tried desperately to turn Gannets into Cory's Shearwaters. It didn't work, so a snooze in the car seemed a better idea. That didn't work either, so I wandered around the town for a while.

As he does in these situations, Old Father Time seemed to be wading through a deep pool of treacle and his forward progress was almost imperceptible. Inevitably though, he made it to the other side and we made our way to the quayside. The nice lady was not there. Terrified perhaps, she may have recalled the 'Man with No Name' and was convinced that it was him she had seen earlier that day; more likely, her shift had ended and she had simply gone home to rest. A large man in a very impressive uniform that was on the brink of bursting through the strain of heavy muscles informed us in no uncertain terms that the sailing was again delayed and were told (not asked) to return at 2.00 p.m.

I did not want to hurt his feelings so backed away towards the town where a warm sea of anger and frustration washed over me, each wave pumping through my body by a seriously stressed heart. That pounding muscle had not been working efficiently for two years. Every now and then it would stop for a couple of seconds and then thump back to life with a jolt that rocked my whole body and left my skin damp with sweat. To make matters worse, I had recently been diagnosed with high blood pressure and had deliberately missed my last check-up for fear of what I might be told. At the time, I did not mention this to my friend, as I think it would have worried him to the point of abandoning the expedition there and then. To me that was not an option. I called Nessie and shouted like a maniac down the phone when describing our plight. People in the street turned and gaped in open-mouthed astonishment and Jason tried his best to calm me down. We were going to miss the pelagic trip from St Mary's that evening; that seemed almost certain. There was another the following day, but would they get that bloody boat fixed? Would one trip be enough to catch all the birds I needed? Jason looked completely dejected and embarrassed at my ravings – what on earth was he thinking? What, I thought, if Lee gets all the pelagic species and I can't even get on the sea?

This last scenario would have meant the end of the game for me and, emotionally, I was getting dragged out of control. 'IF this' and 'what IF that' were events that were out of my control and, in any case, they had not yet even happened. I recalled an old expression my grandfather used to use when I was a small boy questioning 'ifs' and 'what ifs'. His big ruddy face would look down at me seriously and say, 'Lad, if yer anti 'ad balls she'd be yer uncle, so gerron wi' yer 'nittin''. Sensible as this advice was, it comforted me little. Nessie was equally philosophical with her suggestion that at least Jason and I could have some 'fun' while we were away, 'you know – a lads night out, sort of thing'. My reply was forceful, business-like and pivotal. 'Ness, I'm not here to have "fun". I'm here to get these f***ing birds!'

Meanwhile, Jason was on the phone to his partner Suzie. He was calmer but was starting to surf on my wave of near-hysteria.

He was still in command of himself though, and even managed to laugh a couple of times during their conversation. This irritated me hugely and I asked him what on earth could be funny about this desperate situation. He told me that Suzie expected me to buy one of those kids' inflatable plastic toy crocodiles and paddle to the Scillies and that on no account was he to do the same. Good idea as it was, my inability to swim made it a poor option. However, Suzie's simple comic observation was like a breath of cool, sane air in a roasting asylum. Instantly she defused the situation and we sat giggling like a couple of schoolboys over our pints of local ale.

Soon an official from the Steamship Company came into the pub and gave the 'thumbs up' sign that meant that *finally* we were on our way. Anger and frustration gave way to relief and the hope that we would make the evening's pelagic trip. But the police officers who sauntered up the quay had other ideas. Apparently, some idiot had got himself drunk and was creating merry hell about the ship not leaving on time and, unfortunately, was still belligerently on board. Perhaps understandably, he was by now reluctant to leave but leave he had to – even if it took two burly coppers to persuade him. Yet another delay. It was now certain that we were going to miss *The Kingfisher*, though at least we were on our way.

We grabbed the best sea-watching vantage point we could find and set sail across that small, yet significant piece of the Atlantic Ocean. As we did so, I noticed a gaggle of birders atop the cliffs of Porthgwarra and, distantly through my binoculars, felt sure that I could make out the form of Lee Evans. Since there were no noteworthy sea birds in sight, I assumed he was having another bad day.

At about 4.00 p.m., I noticed a storm-petrel on the starboard side of the ship. It was gliding for long periods and its flight was not at all bat-like in the manner of a European Storm-petrel. Its wings were long and there was no white bar on the

Chapter 7

underwings. At a distance of 200 metres and for approximately three minutes, it flew alongside the ship and afforded good views to both Jason and I. We agreed then and there that we were watching a Wilson's Storm-petrel. Much punching of the air ensued until my pager sent a message that a 'Wilson's Petrel' had been seen off Porthgwarra a little while earlier. We both knew who was claiming it but were mystified as to how anyone could identify such a bird at what had to be extreme distance. We simply shook our heads and decided that it was impossible. Whoever it was had to be stringing everyone along – or simply 'stringing' as birders say. A few Cory's Shearwaters were also reported and we wondered about these too.

Apart from our obvious joy with the Wilson's Storm-petrel, our sailing was uneventful save for three Manx Shearwaters that graced us with their majestic presence. As we approached St Mary's harbour, *The Kingfisher* was setting sail and ruefully we watched her depart. I waved to her as we crossed but do not think she recognized me. We had our 'Wilson's' – the biggest target of the trip – and, despite the traumas of the day, we were pretty happy.

I did not want Lee to know where I was, as he would still have time to get to St Mary's for the following evening's pelagic trip. So I decided not to report our petrel to RBA until it was too late for him to catch up with us. I understand now that his planned pelagic trip on board *The Scillonian* had been cancelled (presumably for the very same engine faults that had delayed us) and this gave me a huge advantage. I was not about to give it away. I wondered how desperate someone might be to claim a Wilson's Storm-petrel and a Cory's Shearwater if his best means of getting to see such creatures was stranded in harbour. On a couple of occasions my phone rang and the word 'Lee' came up on the display. I chose not to answer. I had already decided just exactly how desperate he might be.

Finding accommodation was a nightmare. In my stupidity I

had not bothered to book a bed and breakfast for the night as I thought it would be easy enough to find it in such a tourist-oriented place. Unfortunately, St Mary's was full of tourists and there was no room at any of the inns. We ended up staying in an expensive hotel. The manager took pity on such bedraggled apparitions and let us stay for a very reasonable price – particularly upon discovering that Jason and I did not want breakfast. A quick splash under the tap, a long stretch of joint-cracking exercises and a cup of coffee were all that were needed to send us on our way to The Scillonian Club. There friendly faces would surely greet us. The one face I hoped not to see was fortunately not there, and we left for our room pleasantly relaxed. After a wee dram of Scottish nectar, slumber called from the soft pillows as invitingly as the smell of roast lamb on a Sunday afternoon. As a final irony, *The Kingfisher* was not employed on a birding trip that evening but was out shark fishing instead.

On the following day we were in Tresco, wishing our lives away until *The Kingfisher* was due to set sail. There was little there to keep our interest, though Jason did find a Pied Flycatcher. The most noteworthy event arrived as I put my hand to my belt in search of my phone and found that it was not there. Much soul-searching discussion had resulted in the decision to let the cat out of the bag regarding my whereabouts. Losing my means of contact with the outside world at this particular time was therefore extremely frustrating. Jason had the bright idea of calling my number, whereupon we would retrace our steps until the phone was found by listening for its ring. We set the cunning plan in motion and proceeded across the island, listening intently for the strains of Leeds United's anthem *Marching On Together* (my ring tone at the time) from the bracken. March we did, but thankfully not for long. The machine was relocated fairly quickly, much to our relief, since passers-by were becoming ever more alarmed at our antics. I was

Chapter 7

reminded of the final scene in the film of that wonderful old sitcom *Dad's Army* where the brave men of the Warmington-on-Sea platoon were warned of a Nazi plot to tunnel beneath the English Channel. As the camera retreated, the viewer was left watching Mainwaring, Pike, Wilson and Jones with their ears to the cliff top turf, listening for the sounds of digging.

I later rang Tom at RBA and made some lame excuse (which clearly he did not believe) for not reporting the Wilson's Storm-petrel earlier, thereby releasing a huge weight of conscience from my shoulders. We then set off back to St Mary's and the climax of a trip we had looked forward to for many months but which, on several occasions, had looked doomed to failure. Back on the main island we spent a while relaxing and looking out to sea from The Garrison. A Meadow Brown butterfly floated past; it was not until later that I realized it belonged to a distinct subspecies endemic to the Isles of Scilly. Jason found a small cockroach that had apparently never been recorded before on St Mary's, whilst I, unimpressed, ran through the latest messages on my pager. The roller-coaster journey took yet another twist, as Booted and Melodious Warblers were present at Portland in Dorset. Lee was surely onto them already, and there was nothing I could do about it. I 'knew' he would claim Wilson's Storm-petrel and Cory's Shearwater from Porthgwarra and he had almost certainly seen the other, more common, target bird – Great Shearwater – from the very same cliffs. This would leave him two birds ahead with two more available. By the time I could get to Dorset, it was almost certain that one, if not both, of the warblers would have gone, thus leaving me in serious debt. The ranting started again, and my tenure in the real world seemed fragile. Despondent, I trudged to the harbour, whilst Jason, as ever mystified, followed behind.

The Kingfisher lay alongside the harbour wall in readiness to depart. An orderly queue formed at her side. Amongst the expectant passengers were a couple of lads who had been standing with Lee and the assembled sea-watchers at Porthgwarra the previous day. They did not know of my attempt to win the title that year, or even who I was, and so spoke openly of the events that had taken place. Apparently, the petrel in question was a mile and a half distant, and the views of Cory's Shearwater were shared by no one else. As I listened to the conversation I was tempted to join in but, in the circumstances, wisely made no comment.

In retrospect, I think it was not so much a case of wisdom as shock. Many of the people who spoke that evening doubted some of Lee's claims. In a way I was relieved, as, from then on, the man's almost mythical aura, which I had held in reverence for so long, slowly dissipated into the ether. It was the dawn of a realization that Lee was not *special* after all. He was just an ordinary bloke with ordinary faults and the same ordinary temptations were bound to cross his mind. Don't misunderstand me; I was furious at the prospect that my rival might not be entirely trustworthy and terribly upset that I had bestowed so much trust where perhaps it was not deserved. I remembered the many occasions on which I had defended Lee from derisory attacks, which, at the time, I believed were borne simply of jealousy and I cringed at my apparent gullibility. However, I now knew that I was not batting against the 'Awesome Aussie' Shane Warne but merely a good county standard leg-spinner. What is more, the rough outside my leg stump created on the orders of the main strike bowler had been removed and the pitch was now even and flat. In fact, it may even be starting to favour the batsman.

As *The Kingfisher* was getting ready to sail, Jason decided that he needed a pee and headed off to the quayside Gents. Frankly, I could not believe it, as we were here for one purpose and it was not to urinate at the point of departure. I boarded the boat without him and we were ready to set sail. Still no Jason!

'Hang on a minute!' I shouted to the skipper.

Chapter 7

'He'd better get a move on!' was Alec's reply.

The Kingfisher released her moorings and pulled away from the harbour wall, ever anxious to be on her way.

'Here he is!' I pleaded, and Alec, bless him, repositioned his boat to take him on board. Never have I met a luckier Welshman. I reminded him of 'Riley's Rule Number One'.

We sailed over the depths of the warm northern Atlantic Ocean in search of a bird that breeds in the chill of Antarctica. The familiar Isles of Scilly grew ever smaller as we bucked and rolled over the vast sea to an invisible field where our dreams were waiting for harvest. A 'blue' Fulmar crossed our wake and I began to realize that I was indeed in a very special place.

Watching seabirds from the land can often be extremely frustrating as they are usually very distant, and an inexpert eye can find it almost impossible to identify them correctly. I wonder how many birders have ticked shearwaters and petrels from their 'want' list without *really* seeing them. There is rarely the opportunity to study plumage characters in detail. I know many people who simply regard sea-watching as a necessary evil. The only satisfactory way to appreciate these creatures is to actually get on to the sea and get amongst them.

As we ploughed through the water, there were long periods where no birds were visible and an electric sense of anticipation crackled in the air. Then suddenly, a Great Shearwater would appear as if from nowhere. Gasps of relief and wonder could be heard around the boat as the stately animal powered effortlessly on rigid wings, almost to within touching distance across our wake. Around the boat it would soar until, deciding that nothing was to be gained by staying, away it would accelerate without any apparent means of propulsion. Low across the waves with wing tips kissing the water, it would glide into the evening and, as suddenly as it appeared, was gone. In contrast, an occasional Great Skua would drive past with powerful wing-beats that seemed to struggle to keep their owner aloft. These birds took little notice of *The Kingfisher*, and most of those aboard took little notice of them.

Mysteriously to us, Alec decided that we had reached the right spot and stopped the engine. Although I was with several other people, I felt strangely alone. No one spoke as we drifted aimlessly and silently in that vast ocean, and I could sense the souls of long-lost sailors beckoning me from their watery graves. As evening drew in, the pastel air enveloped us. A liquid atmosphere of soft pinks and blues caressed us and then flowed into the heavy green and purple of the monstrous pond on which we sat. In the far distance, small lights twinkled, but so disoriented was I that I had no idea whence they came.

Foul-smelling 'chum' in the form of decomposing fish was dropped over the side of the boat, swiftly followed by the baited hooks of the shark anglers who were with us, their freshly caught mackerels suspended beneath gaudy balloons. I hoped we would not 'need a bigger boat' as Chief Brody had observed in the film *Jaws*. Somewhere in the twilight, tiny noses sniffed the odours of decaying fish and, unbeknown to us, small black bat-like birds approached from downwind. A call of 'Petrel!' broke the spell that enchanted me and all eyes were on the little bird as it weaved a path around us from the filaments of the gentle air.

It was a European Storm-petrel – not the species we were hoping for but delightful nonetheless. Like many birders, I had only ever seen these birds at great distance, sometimes as far away as a mile, in the form of a barely perceptible black dot. Here I could see all the taxonomic characteristics which make a 'Stormy'. Others soon followed it, and the expectancy grew as we waited for their rarer cousin. An efficient and unexcited call from behind me proclaimed its presence, and there it was. Bob Flood has seen so many Wilson's Storm-petrels that to him they are almost commonplace. I was pleased that he with his expertise was on board for, even at such close quarters, these birds can tax one's identification skills. Adeptly, he took us through the distinguishing features. By the time others of its kind arrived, we all knew exactly what to look for. Jason and I discussed the bird we had seen from *The Scillonian* the previous day and decided that we had indeed seen a Wilson's Storm-petrel. Those nagging little doubts that all honest birders should feel were gone. By the time darkness fell, we had seen at least six of these scarce birds and possibly more. Silently we headed back to shore, everyone seemingly exhausted from the experience but eminently satisfied. Tomorrow, Jason and I were to leave the magical islands, hoping that those warblers were still at Portland. In the meantime, I still needed to see a Cory's Shearwater and was disappointed that I had not done so thus far.

A tinge of sadness was evident as we set sail for the mainland but we hoped to see many birds on the journey, including the warblers at Portland. Hopefully there was plenty of excitement to come, though it was highly unlikely that we would reach Portland before dark. This could give our two little friends yet another opportunity to leave as both species migrate at night. Tense times lay ahead. Thankfully, the return sailing was more eventful than the outward trip. We were entertained by several Manx and a single Sooty Shearwater, two Great Skuas and a European Storm-petrel. This was our last chance to find a Fea's Petrel and it ended in failure. However, our quest for Cory's Shearwaters was more successful as two passed by the stern of the ship: not great views, but good enough. All, bar Fea's Petrel, were now in the bag and, as I knew that Lee had not seen one either, I started to feel a little more relaxed. Back on *terra firma* the headlong rush for Portland began. Unfortunately, this was in vain, as darkness descended well before we reached our target.

As we approached Weymouth, Jason's phone rang and an obviously heated discussion ensued. Clearly it was Suzie at the other end and she was evidently unhappy about something. Jason later told me that she was convinced he was drunk and that our couple of days away was turning into an excuse for a booze-up. In hindsight, I can understand why she may have thought so. We were both so physically and mentally drained that Jason was slurring his words and did indeed sound drunk. It took several calls to convince her that this was not the case, but all ended well. When eventually we did reach Portland, the night was pitch black and the sky clear. The conditions were in fact perfect for migration, and my hopes of seeing the warblers the following morning were sinking fast. Had Suzie called again an hour or so later she would have had every reason for suspicion, as we did some fairly severe damage to a bottle of Scotch, which Jason had secreted about his person. That it was served in a plastic mug, which was unwashed after holding many strong black coffees, mattered not a jot; rather, it was just what was needed to round off an exhausting day.

Jason seemed to sleep well, but I was by now regularly getting bouts of insomnia, and tonight was one of those nights when Morpheus, god of sleep, no matter how much I begged him, simply would not come. The hours before dawn crawled by like an aged cripple. Brief catnaps were punctuated by long periods of anxiety and self-examination, bordering on paranoia. I needed to be at home with my wife, I needed home comforts and needed to relax. But, in the darkness of the sleeping *Enterprise*, what I felt I needed most were those two little birds. My priorities were starting to become dangerously illogical.

Thankfully, dawn eventually arrived and the task in hand snapped me out of my waking nightmare. Fairly soon we were onto a Melodious Warbler and my confidence soared. A chance meeting with someone who looked authoritative taught us something about the habits of the Booted Warbler and we quickly decided on the best vantage point overlooking a patch of rough vegetation where the bird had regularly been seen. To our utter amazement, I found the bird within seconds of beginning the search, and about half a dozen of us were delighted by the views we were afforded by this very scarce species. The muscles in my face were fixed into a grin so wide that it hurt. After the usual obligatory hugs and handshakes, we went to the observatory to watch a second Melodious Warbler before setting a course for Norfolk. 'Make it so, Number One. Let's go home!'

By the end of August, I had reached 342 species. However, Lee had irritated me enough with his claims of Wilson's Storm-petrel, Cory's Shearwater and, in my view most ludicrous of all, his unilateral decision to accept the Hooded Merganser (in the knowledge that I had not seen it) that I decided around this time that I should play by his own rules and 'accept' the Suffolk Bufflehead. Such little regard did I now have for Lee's authority that I considered it to be of no more importance than my own. Hence I amended my own total to 343.

September – getting personal

September in Norfolk can be wonderful for scarce birds, and 2002 was certainly no disappointment. Against a backdrop of what one might call 'lesser celebrities', such as Red-backed Shrike (my first for the year), Barred Warbler, Curlew Sandpiper and many Sooty Shearwaters, we were entertained by Red-breasted Flycatchers at Wells and Weybourne, at least one Icterine Warbler, a Ring-necked Parakeet at Old Hunstanton and a 'Continental' Coal Tit at Stiffkey. On an unsuccessful trudge along Blakeney Point in search of a Short-toed Lark, I was privileged to be a part of the uncovering of a Great Snipe. Not that I had anything to do with finding this rare and elusive creature but I did flush the vegetation with tremendous enthusiasm when told to by Richard Millington and Steve Gantlett. Unfortunately for me, Lee was also accidentally in on the act and so I missed a wonderful opportunity to 'get one over' my rival. I remember Nessie phoning by chance at the time and my telling her that 'all was fair in love and war', a comment that made Mr Gantlett grin like a Cheshire cat.

A White-rumped Sandpiper finally appeared nearer home, at Titchwell in fact, but the crazy deed of driving to Cleveland for one had already been done, and the thought that Lee was probably sniggering into his chips did little to calm my irritation.

On the 27th, a splendid male Sardinian Warbler was found at Old Hunstanton, and I thanked the God of Twitching that I lived so close. I arrived before the hordes to find a handful of delighted birders gazing upon a truly magnificent bird. The pastel tones of grey, the intense black head and that piercing red eye made a sight to cheer the hardest of hearts. I returned home a happy man. I was even happier when I discovered later that

Chapter 8

evening that Lee had missed the bird and would have to return the following day. In the darker recesses of my soul I was really beginning to enjoy his failures, though, in hindsight, I am genuinely ashamed to admit it.

On the 9th a huge fall of migrants arrived; Stiffkey Woods seemed to be bouncing with them. Ian Burrows and I saw upwards of 30 Pied and 20 Spotted Flycatchers, as well as innumerable other 'bits and pieces'. Flushed with excitement, we determined to visit Holkham Woods the next day to see what had taken refuge there. We set off early on the 10th and made our way studiously through the pines, but little was there to greet us. We were disappointed and dismayed as we thought we had read our weather forecasts to perfection and, bearing in mind the rewards of the previous afternoon, were expecting great things. Had the previous day been slightly less spectacular, we would perhaps have been pleased with the few flycatchers we found but we were not. Still, there were the dunes to come at the western end and, who knows? Maybe a shrike would be waiting for us. It was not. Like Laurel and Hardy, we scratched our heads in puzzlement '...*another fine mess...*'. As the scratching intensified, I heard an unfamiliar high-pitched '*pseeeeet*' call from behind me. On turning, I saw a small pipit fly into the dunes to the north of the pine trees and immediately thought, 'Oh, well, that was that.' However, Ian came over and was delighted that I actually saw where the bird went as he too heard the call and said: 'If I didn't know better, I'd have said that was a Red-throated Pipit.'

We decided to try to find it and headed into the dunes where we were immediately greeted by a very obliging Wryneck. We enjoyed the bird for a while but our concentration was soon interrupted by that same call and, looking up, we saw our quarry flying by and calling clearly at close quarters. Ian confirmed without doubt that it was indeed a Red-throated Pipit. Abroad, Ian is very familiar with the species and recognized it within seconds. It landed ahead of us in the dunes, but, try as we might, we could not relocate it. Whilst searching for the pipit, we were amazed to find yet another Wryneck. We looked at each other in disbelief at our fantastic, but (we felt) well-earned luck. A third phone call was made to RBA. By now, they must surely have begun to doubt our integrity. Imagine their response to the fourth one then.

Within minutes of reporting the second Wryneck, I was absolutely staggered to find myself watching a Camberwell Beauty butterfly gliding along the track. I have been 'into' butterflies for well over thirty years and had never before seen one of these scarce vagrants from Scandinavia. As I sank to my knees in wonderment I asked Ian to tell me that I was not dreaming. With his rarely-stirred air of calmness, he told me that I was not and ordered me back on my feet. We followed the beautiful insect into the dunes where we watched it for several minutes whereupon it crawled into a Marram tussock, perhaps with the intention of going straight into hibernation. This would not be unusual behaviour for a butterfly of this type, as Peacocks, which are related, do so fairly soon after the emergence of the summer generation. We marked the spot for future reference just as a ridiculously low fly-over by a military helicopter sent all the birds in the area spinning to the four winds. Thus ended any prospect of further views of our pipit. We made our way home in a somewhat trance-like state and, in time-honoured fashion, celebrated lavishly that evening.

Twitches during September were rather few and far between, though not without controversy. On the 2nd, I spent several hours traipsing around Bole Plantation in Yorkshire before getting acceptable flight views of a Two-barred Crossbill. It was evident that the bird had only one wing-bar, but what a bar it was! This was clearly no Common Crossbill because the large white patch was bright, broad and clearly defined. Everybody who was there at the time was satisfied that we had seen the Two-barred Crossbill, and so I rang the sighting in to

Chapter 8

RBA. Shortly after, Lee rang with his decision that it was a Common Crossbill. He had not seen the bird in question and therefore, in my opinion, could not sensibly come to such a conclusion. (I was later proved to be correct, as a second wing-bar was observed growing over a period of time when the bird moulted.) His imperious edicts were beginning to get on my nerves.

The following day was spent with Lee and Nessie in Cornwall where we were successful in finding a Gull-billed Tern at Drift reservoir. We also saw a bunting-like bird at Nanjizal Valley. An Ortolan Bunting had been seen there the previous day, but our bird was distant, silhouetted and brief in appearance. I felt that it could have been just about anything and to claim Ortolan Bunting for it would be folly, if not dishonest. Lee was reticent about the matter and did not seem to want to discuss it. Our luck with ortolans changed later in the day though, as up to three were reported at Tore Common. Off we charged and we were rewarded with wonderful views of at least two of these scarce birds. A Red-backed Shrike provided a cameo, and we dipped a Rose-coloured Starling on our way home. On arriving at Lee's house, there seemed to be genuine affection in his hug and his kiss for Nessie, and I wondered if my waning opinion of him was perhaps a little harsh. Either way, a competition was still afoot. I was delighted to see a Glossy Ibis at Budleigh Salterton in Devon (a species which had put me in arrears, as Lee had seen it in Oxfordshire a few days previously) and a charmingly coy Greenish Warbler in the depths of Lincolnshire at a place with the equally charming name of Donna Nook. Exactly a week later, I was furious with myself to discover that my opinion of Lee had not been nearly harsh enough.

On the 14th, I drove to Rye Meads in Hertfordshire for a Solitary Sandpiper. This is a very rare bird indeed and could not be missed. I guessed that Lee had already seen it, and clearly this increased the necessity for success. One can imagine my relief on seeing a pager message, confirming the continued presence of the bird, and I headed for the site with calm confidence. On reaching the hide, I discovered Lee ushering small groups of birders inside from what was clearly going to develop into a considerable queue. Jokingly, he refused me admission, and we exchanged pleasantries for a short while until my turn came to view the bird. I couldn't stay long, as many people were eagerly waiting their chance and so I left quickly to let them through.

On leaving the hide, Lee asked of my plans for the rest of the day. I explained that I was going to Ferrybridge in Dorset for the Semipalmated Sandpiper. He was very excited about this and asked if he and his friend could join me. I guessed he would probably go there anyway so there was no point in being awkward and I agreed. At least it would reduce the petrol cost.

On our way there, he grilled me incessantly about the Glossy Ibis. 'Exactly where was it?' 'What time were you there?' 'Who else was there?' 'What bridge?' 'What river?' From his tone I sensed that he simply did not believe that I had seen the bird, and his attitude was making me very angry.

I stewed on it all day and I felt like a pressure cooker that was about to explode. This was the final straw. I decided then and there that the game would now get personal. I was no longer going to aim to win the competition – I wanted to beat Lee Evans. Winning was secondary.

Ian and I had been planning something of a coup for several weeks. So far as I was aware, Lee had no intentions of going to the northern isles this year ('the weather's always awful and the chips are terrible') and, favourable weather permitting, it was possible that I could score pretty heavily should I go to the Shetlands. Ian had several helpful contacts and had worked the islands himself on several occasions. I had never been to these islands and was somewhat daunted by the prospect of birding such an unknown, vast and remote area – particularly as the

Chapter 8

pager would almost certainly not receive messages there.

That little grey box had become my closest friend. Ten days without it seemed unimaginable. However, my mobile phone would be a good means of communication with which to keep in touch not only with any rarities available in the islands but, perhaps more importantly, with events on the mainland. I would also have the help of Paul Harvey whose knowledge of the islands and their birds is immense. My greatest weapon though, was surprise. If Lee was unaware of my plans he would almost certainly not go but if he found out, I felt sure he would want to tag along. Of course, this would defeat the object of the exercise. So, for several weeks, I had to be very careful whom I spoke to on the subject. I spent many hours poring over maps and past issues of journals such as *Birding World*, learning about the topography of the islands and localities where rare birds had previously been found. I also studied the taxonomy of scarce species such as Lanceolated Warbler, Pallas's Grasshopper Warbler and Pechora Pipit, which were likely to occur but would be new to me. With a head full of new information and the good wishes of all involved, I sailed from Aberdeen into the night towards the Shetlands.

In order to cut costs, I decided not to book a cabin on board the ferry but to slum it on any available horizontal surface. Despite having downed several pints of nauseating lager, the engine noise, excitement and sheer discomfort precluded sleep. I don't remember how long the journey took. I think it was fourteen hours, but it seemed like an eternity and I have never felt so impatient in my life. However, the experience was to prove useful as I re-learned a long forgotten ability to simply 'shut down'. It is not exactly sleep and it is not exactly consciousness, but a state wherein the outside world seems far away and time no longer exists. I suppose one might call it a trance, but I'm not sure if that is actually accurate. Whatever it is, I have been able to do it all my life and, on occasions when I have been bored out of my mind, such as during allegedly important departmental meetings or excessively lengthy tench-fishing sessions, it has proved very useful indeed. This was just such an occasion, so I closed my eyes and waited for dawn. When it arrived, I felt refreshed and ready to go. Several skuas, Puffins and Black Guillemots came with it and many stately Gannets bade me 'Good morning'. As always, I had 'butterflies in my stomach' as I waited on the bridge of *The Enterprise* for the ferry doors to open and allow me back on to dry land. What was waiting for me, I wondered? Well, I will tell you: a Black-headed Bunting that had already left and a weather system that looked as promising for producing scarce migrants as Leeds' prospects of winning the Premiership.

The winds were strong and from the west and they were predicted to remain so for the foreseeable future. The landscape was unbelievably barren, and birds of any description were few and far between. I immediately decided that I did not like the place and, within a few birdless hours, I wanted to go home. But I was here and I was damned well going to make the best of it. It was time to roll up my sleeves and get to work.

Birding in the Shetlands can certainly seem daunting for the first-time visitor. However, there is one basic rule and that is to find any tall vegetation, for this is where the birds will be sheltering in an otherwise bleak and often windswept landscape. These refuges can take the form of woodlands such as Kirgord Plantation, though such habitat is rare, gardens like those at the Busta Hotel and the Voxter Centre, small croft gardens (the ones at Loch Tingwall and North Collafirth can be very productive) or any patches of scrub or rank herbage. These last habitats can sometimes be very small but are always worth checking as they may be the only cover for a tired bird for many a mile.

My short stay did not make me an authority on birding here, yet I found that the best tactic was simply to drive around and stop whenever I saw a likely looking spot. There are not many of them so considerable distances have to be covered. Each stop needs only to be a short one, and the day can be ended in the knowledge that one has worked hard and thoroughly. The optimum time for rarities appears to be during the latter half of September and into October. Even if 'heart-stopping' species are absent, there are always common migrants around to help keep the enthusiasm going and one's hopes alive.

Most of my birding was done on Mainland, and my two visits to the more remote islands were made for specific birds. Yet the same basic methods should be a good skeleton on which the new visitor can hang some meat. Even when the odds seemed stacked against you, as they did with me in the midst of seemingly unsuitable weather, a huge surprise can be just around the corner – as on the 24th.

On that morning, the winds had increased in strength and were coming in from more or less the north. I decided to drive to the north of Mainland, look for new areas to work and end up on the coast for some sea-watching, in the hope of finding a Grey Phalarope or a Sabine's gull. On my way I went through North Collafirth and noticed a small croft garden containing what appeared to be a *Brassica* crop, which was surrounded by a sheltering border of mixed deciduous and coniferous trees. It seemed a perfect spot to shelter a weary bird, so I stopped and scanned the vegetation. Almost immediately I saw a *Phylloscopus* warbler feeding in the lower part of a Sycamore. It was only fifteen metres away from me, and I was able to study the bird closely for about half an hour. It took me only a few minutes to identify it as an Arctic Warbler. I had seen this species at very close quarters the previous year in the Isles of Scilly and, only a few days previously, I had been watching its congener, the Greenish Warbler, in Lincolnshire. I therefore had good, clear memories of the taxonomic features of both species and could, without doubt and with great excitement, phone RBA with news of my find. Discovering such a scarce bird was one of the highlights of my year and illustrates well the old maxim – 'The harder you work, the luckier you get.' I found little else of note on Mainland, though great adventures awaited me on trips to Fair Isle and Foula.

I had hoped to get to Fair Isle on my first full day in the islands since a River Warbler was reported to be there. This is an extremely rare species, one which was new to me, and one which Lee was unlikely to see elsewhere. Imagine my frustration when I discovered I could not fly there for another two days. I was sure the bird would have gone by then, but daily calls to Andrew at RBA kept my hopes alive, as it hung on in the tiny garden at the observatory. Perhaps the horrible weather was deterring its departure.

On arrival at the small airfield on the morning of the 23rd, I was told that, despite the poor weather, there would be a flight going out to Fair Isle. However, the conditions were due to worsen and my return that day could not be guaranteed. This did not concern me unduly, as I had no specific plans for the following day and, if the worst came to the worst, I was sure the observatory warden would take pity on me and lend me some floor space on which to sleep for the night.

Off I set with some hastily made butties, a flask of hot water, some coffee and enough Hamlet cigars to last a couple of days. The small aeroplane was delightful. The inside seemed no larger than that of my car, thus making one feel very close to the outside environment and thereby enhancing the sensation of flying. From behind the very friendly pilot, I could see all the controls and watch their manipulation. It seemed very easy indeed, but I decided that this was an illusion created by an expert hand. So expert was that hand and so considerate was its owner of my obvious nervousness, that I soon settled down and enjoyed the flight. From on high I made some mental notes of good-looking habitats that I could later search. Before long, we approached the airstrip on Fair Isle. I was amazed at the wonderful sensation as the tiny craft banked and descended towards the rough ground below. It was only then that I could comprehend the speed at which we were travelling. When aloft, the plane seemed to be labouring along at a snail's pace, but as the heather-clad hills approached, their passing gave a true perspective of our velocity. We were going very fast indeed, and my nerves returned as I wondered how on earth we were going to stop before reaching the end of the runway.

Of course, we did stop and as I disgorged myself from his protection, that pilot became the closest friend I had ever had. Armed with a small map, I trudged unsteadily towards the observatory through some of the bleakest surroundings one could imagine. There seemed to be no features of any note, save the moody mountains, their coarse coats of heather and veins of icy streams. Had the weather been sunny and warm it would doubtlessly have created a very different impression, but today it was simply grim. I was reminded of the two American tourists in the film *An American Werewolf in London* and the advice they were given by the local farmers, 'Stay off the moors, lads'. I was thankful that it was daytime, for at least I would not have to 'Beware the full moon'.

When I reached the observatory I was greeted by one of the staff who, on hearing that it was my first visit, was extremely helpful. He told me how I might find the River Warbler and gave me maps and some literature on the island. These would be very useful later in the day, having hopefully achieved my primary goal. The observatory garden is tiny, and I admit to feeling rather silly watching over such an insignificant patch with such sincere and intense concentration. Had this been anywhere else, I think I would have been too embarrassed to remain for long, but this is Shetland birding for sure. Such places are little safe harbours in an otherwise storm-lashed sea. Moreover, I learned that the River Warbler had already been seen that morning and so my confidence was high. Two Reed Warblers created several false alarms during my wait, but before long, my quarry was in my binoculars, and I had satisfactory views during which I noted the diagnostic scalloped pattern on the undertail coverts. A dull and uninspiring bird it may have been, but it was worth its weight in gold.

The rest of my day in Fair Isle was productive in that I saw several interesting birds, including Lapland Bunting, Barred Warbler and two Common Crossbills feeding on thistles, although at the back of my mind I wondered if the plane would return that day. Feeling extremely weary, I made my way back to the airfield with my fingers crossed and cat-napped for an hour in the small building that served as a waiting room. Several people arrived as the departure time neared, and I felt heartened by their positive demeanour. Some of them had been on the outward journey and asked if I had seen the bird I was after; one even remembered its name. All were pleased that my journey had been successful. I appreciated their kindness but wondered if they were also merely humouring the strange Sassenach in their midst.

Our plane duly arrived to carry us back to Mainland. Feeling less nervous about being in such a small craft and more confident of my newly found friend the pilot, I enjoyed the trip immensely. It was a fairly rough and noisy flight, and I was amused at how smooth and quiet *The Enterprise* seemed in contrast as I drove her back to Lerwick.

I could not get a flight to the Long-billed Dowitcher on the island of Foula until the 25th. So I spent the following day travelling around Mainland, basking in the glory of my sighting of the Arctic Warbler. The wind strength had increased considerably overnight, and I was beginning to worry that my scheduled flight to Foula would be cancelled. I was also worried about what was happening further south, as several rare birds, including Black-headed Bunting, Western Bonelli's Warbler and Buff-breasted Sandpiper, had arrived nearer home.

Chapter 8

During one conversation, Andrew at RBA said forcefully, 'Adrian, you need to get off that island!' Although my confidence was high having found the Arctic Warbler, the prevailing winds were due to change to westerly again, and Andrew's advice seemed sensible. I therefore decided to leave Shetland early, the following day in fact, and so rearranged my ferry sailing back to Aberdeen. On my return from Foula, I would have about forty minutes to get back to Lerwick and board ship. The staff at P&O Ferries were very obliging and agreed to give me plenty of leeway when it came to checking in. All I needed now was for the return flight from Foula to arrive on time.

The weather the following day was wet and very windy and expected to worsen. I arrived at the airfield to be greeted by the news that the outward flight would depart on time. Great news, but what about the return? 'Oh, with the weather as it is, we can't guarantee a return today,' the lady said. What on earth was I to do? I needed that dowitcher. At the moment, I stood to return with just two birds and that was simply not good enough. I would have to take the risk and go to Foula in the hope that the plane would come and get me off.

The flight was extremely rough, but my new friend handled it brilliantly and we got there safely. I asked him what the prospects were of getting back. His reply was a faint smile, a gentle shake of the head and a shrug of his uniformed shoulders. Perhaps he was not a mate after all. Perhaps he was emulating Chief Engineer 'Scottie' of the original *Star Trek* by exaggerating the severity of the situation in order to maintain his reputation as 'miracle-worker'. Either way, I was here now and would simply have to see what dramas were yet to unfold.

It took me about an hour and a half to find the Long-billed Dowitcher by which time I was drenched. A bonus Pectoral Sandpiper did not make me feel any drier. I was wearing waterproof clothing, but it was of poor quality, and the wind was driving the rain so hard that it found its way through the tiniest gaps. It was running down my back in icy rivulets. The jeans beneath my over-trousers were soaked where the water had simply forced its way through. I was thoroughly miserable and, to make matters worse, could not find the Yellow-browed Warbler that would have given me a fourth tick to take home. I sat on a rock and pondered on the predicament. I had something like four hours to wait for the plane – assuming it came at all. If it did not, I had nowhere to stay for the night and saw little chance of finding somewhere in that inhospitable landscape.

I had two apples, a small bottle of water, three cigars and a phone that had very little charge left in it. Thankfully there was a reasonable signal. Soaked to the skin, I was getting colder by the minute. I decided that not only was this a difficult situation but potentially a very dangerous one. I made my way back to the airstrip, where, thankfully, the door to the waiting room (actually a small shed) was open. There I could escape the wind and rain. On the wall was a phone number for the emergency services should the onset of hypothermia demand it. I was shivering uncontrollably, and the latter scenario was beginning to seem less like over-dramatization and more like a distinct possibility. Running on the spot for a while increased my body temperature to the point where the shivering stopped; however, I was concerned that my waterproof clothing was not going to give the rest of my clothes a chance to dry. I took off my leggings and watched satisfied as steam rose from my jeans. It soon became apparent that this was a bad idea, as within a couple of minutes my legs were icily cold. Back on went the waterproofs. They too were icily cold and I was beginning to think there was no way I could win. A look at the clock on my phone was of little comfort, and the two bars on the battery meter did little to bolster my confidence.

Earlier in the day, I saw the remains of cars on what one might describe as the front lawns of the few crofts in the island. In various states of decay they lay; some recent and turning

Chapter 8

brown, the oldest mere orange stains in the grass with just the hardest parts (I suppose one might call them the skeletons) remaining. A gearbox, transmission housing and circles of rubber were all that were left – the ghosts of someone's former pride and joy. I supposed there were no 'scrappies' out here. When a vehicle had outlived its usefulness it was simply left to rot alongside its replacement. In a bizarre moment of madness, I wondered how I was going to look by the time someone found me. I hoped fancifully that my replacement was there in search of a rarer bird than a Long-billed Dowitcher, and that he or she would look kindly on the stain that was their forerunner.

It was time to phone Nessie and this I did to tell her of my predicament and, most importantly, to tell her not to waste what little charge I had left by phoning me back to see how I was. This was a forlorn hope, as she was extremely worried and continued to call regularly. One bar left and I resorted to shouting into the phone in an attempt to stop her. I turned the phone off and felt very lonely indeed.

Shivering again, hungry and without nicotine and caffeine, I remembered my experience on the ferry and decided it was time to 'shut down'. Stiffness occasionally stirred me and I woke to greet a tremulous body and faraway mind. I recalled being lowered into a deep hole with Nessie looking down from beside a one-eyed man wearing a crucifix in his ear. In silence I was screaming that he could not have seen a Long-billed Dowitcher that year and that I had won against the odds or the most ultimate of consequences. I felt strangely satisfied despite the fact that I was clearly being laid dead into my grave. I have never felt the same about birding since and hopefully shall never again. These horrible images lived briefly and haunted that land between consciousness and sleep, a land where the boundaries dividing dream and reality are broad and grey. To hell with Major Tom, I needed any bloody pilot! Time to 'shut down' again. How I hoped I was going to get the chance to miss this place. '*Here comes the rain again...*' (Eurythmics). But I was running out of new emotions – I had used them all up.

My regained ability to 'shut down' was rewarded by the discovery that the plane was due in just a few minutes. To this day, I shall never know where those hours went and I suspect it will be only in my most final seconds that I shall find out.

Several people had gathered at the airstrip and things seemed promising for the return of my friend the pilot. I must have looked an absolute fright, as no one wanted to look me in the eye. '*We are the Goon Squad and we're coming to town...*' (David Bowie). All I wanted was a plane, not conversation. Looking up, I saw a tiny light heading my way and, grinning like the cat that got the cream, I realized salvation was on its way. By now, I was back in the land of the sane and, despite having endured a potentially life-threatening situation, logistics became my greatest concern. I had a ferry to catch that would get me closer to a Black-headed Bunting, a Buff-breasted Sandpiper, a Richard's Pipit and a Grey Phalarope – four ticks and at least as many hundred miles to drive.

The light metamorphosed into an aeroplane and, gallantly, it swooped raptor-like onto the rough runway. In a trice I was aboard, and in seconds we were away. I slept a deep sleep for the short duration of the flight and felt almost hominid by the time we landed in Mainland Shetland. As I piped myself aboard *The Enterprise* I realized what a bloody fool I had been – all for the sake of a minor celebrity like a Long-billed Dowitcher. But it was a tick. My ship glided smoothly and rapidly towards Lerwick and, with just five minutes to spare, I steered her onto the ferry that would carry me south towards *terra cognita*. Plot a course, Number One... Engage!

On arrival in Aberdeen, I was greeted with the news that the bunting had departed. Worse still, Lee had seen it. Better news was that he had not seen the Bonelli's Warbler at Pendeen, a bird I knew had already left and was no longer available to me. How I

Chapter 8

wished I had a full complement of crew aboard *The Enterprise*. I was reduced to bawling orders at myself as we sped towards England, and it was not the same as bouncing jocularities off Jason, Phil or Richard. How I longed for a small Welshman, a fellow entomologist or an eminently sensible councillor with whom to share re-entry into dear 'Old Blighty'. As I passed the sign welcoming me to England I felt it had been placed there just for me and that everyone in my fair land was glad to have me home. Sentimentality sated, I planned my next move.

Actually, little planning was needed. All I had to do was to pilot *The Enterprise* fast and south. The Buff-breasted Sandpiper was now the priority, and I would therefore head for Wheldrake Ings in Yorkshire. En route, I would have to keep tabs on an elusive Richard's Pipit and take any opportunities that presented themselves. As it turned out they were few, becoming fewer and, by the time a decision had to be made regarding detours, it seemed sensible to ignore the bird altogether, as too much time was likely to be wasted for probably no gain. On then to Wheldrake where I was to behave in a shameful manner.

The Buff-breasted Sandpiper is a very scarce vagrant to these shores and I know many birders who have not seen one. On arrival at the site, I jumped from the car, trained my binoculars on the bird, satisfied myself that it was indeed the one I wanted and sped off again. I left that beautiful bird without so much as 'by your leave'. I appreciated it not one iota; it was merely a 'tick'. I was more interested in getting the Grey Phalarope at Titchwell. I hope that all my readers never fall into this abyss of insensitivity.

The Richard's Pipit did not show again, and I smirked at my own cleverness and the knowledge that Lee had probably not seen it either. My attitude was getting uglier by the minute. Several hours later I was back in Norfolk and, in the gathering gloom, watched the silver spinning phalarope as it hunted for invertebrates on the water's surface. As I did so I was aware of people casting uneasy glances in my direction. I can only imagine what a mess I looked and so thought it best to head for home lest I frighten the small children. Later that evening I took a hot bath and fell into a doze within its comforting arms. I woke with a start, splashing water in every direction as I found myself once again in that dark hole looking up at Nessie as she laughed ferociously at Lee. How strange are the games played by an exhausted mind; how wonderful was my bed that night; how glad I am that those nightmares have now gone for good. I was reaching a point of no return and metamorphosing into a cold collector of ticks. Little would bother me from now on and, after a good night's sleep, I would be aching for the next challenge.

I was far removed from the person who began the year and yet further from the one who was to finish it. Lee had already seen to that. My tally was now on 357 – probably not quite good enough, but I could always call on that Bufflehead should childishness dictate.

Sea-watching off St. Mary's, Isles of Scilly, with Richard Bromilow. Photo by Phil Gould

The Burren, County Clare. Choughs are seen regularly near the coast, it is also home to many endemic subspecies of butterfly. Photo by the author.

European Storm-petrel
All photos by Gary Thoburn

Red-throated Pipit

Glossy Ibis

White-rumped Sandpiper

Burren Grayling
Photo by the author

Camberwell Beauty
Photo by Robert Thompson

Speckled Wood
Photo by the author

Small Red-eyed Damselfly. Sculthorpe Moor, Norfolk. A recent arrival to Britain that is now well established at many sites in southern England. Photo by the author

Savi's Warbler
All photos by Gary Thoburn

Squacco Heron

European Bee-eater

Killdeer

Huddled against the Norfolk winter: Jason Chapman, Gary Thoburn and the author scan a flock of scoters off Holkham. Photo by Phil Gould

Jason Chapman and the author celebrating the winning total in The Cross Keys, Harpenden. January, 2003. Photo by Suzannah Chapman

October – the Scilly season

How well I remember having a conversation with my friends from Liverpool, Karen and Dave Leeming. Unfortunately, I cannot recall exactly when it took place, but the content proved to be pivotal in my life. The reader, having come on my quest this far with me, will already be aware of my love for Scotland and the joy springtime there brings me. Karen, in her very cultured Scouse accent, told me that, 'bairds or no bairds', the Isles of Scilly are so beautiful that 'Dave and I would go just for the sheer pleasure of being there'. My first visit followed shortly afterwards and I have never looked back – save for some wonderful memories.

That first stay was with Nessie and was spent in a very cramped, but cosy tent at the Garrison campsite. Of course, the weather was abominable, as one might expect on the Atlantic coast in October, but I can honestly say that I had never before enjoyed a holiday so much. The air of camaraderie amongst the birders was tangible. I was somewhat concerned that Nessie would find the atmosphere daunting, this being her first ever 'serious' birding extravaganza; she handled it with great aplomb. In her inimitable fashion, she identified the occasion as a male-dominated affair and therefore appealed to the assembled drones by displaying her ample bosom behind an eye-catching blouse. Once attention had been captured, she charmed everyone with her 'Nessieness' and was also able to maintain birding conversation for, by now, her expertise was growing.

Sadly, but in hindsight predictably, the ladies involved did not quite appreciate her assets and a rather hostile atmosphere emanated from the feminine quarter. Nessie being Nessie, ensured that the following evening was spent by everyone enjoying a few drinks together rather than re-enacting the shoot-out at the OK Corral. Steve Young, the excellent photographer from Liverpool (and a no mean pool player, so it is said) summed up the situation admirably when he asked Nessie, 'Why do you wear all those rings on your right hand?' On hearing the reply 'Because I lead with that hand', he simply said, 'Oh, you're the woman I've heard about. Here, you'd better have these photos for free.'

As we prepared to leave the islands that year, Ray Turley, the great Kentish birder and a wonderfully laid-back guy, gave Nessie a kiss on the cheek and asked if she would be back the following year as '...you certainly know how to make an impression.'

In 2002, I was there without her. The place seemed less alive in her absence, but Richard Bromilow, Phil Gould and Stuart Ford joined me. It was this year that I also forged a valued friendship with Gary Thoburn, an extremely sharp birder from Bristol and expert Tommy Cooper impressionist, whose photos of rare birds appear ever more frequently on the internet. He was very supportive during what was to prove a difficult time on the islands, but more of that later.

On the 1st of October, I visited the Cotswold Water Park in Wiltshire where an elusive eclipse-plumaged male Blue-winged Teal had been reported. As I recall, it was the first of its species to be found that year and, consequently, it attracted much attention, particularly from Lee. I spent a gruelling six hours in search of that duck and was rewarded when a fellow masochist shouted that he had it in his binoculars. Fleet of foot, I caught it in my 'scope and, although my view was brief, I could confirm its identity and triumphantly rang in our finding to RBA.

Within minutes my phone rang and the word 'Lee' appeared on the screen. I ignored it. He was the last person I wanted to speak to. He rang again. And again. I was now so 'pumped up' (thanks for that, John McEnroe) that I decided to

Chapter 9

answer the call. I could hardly believe the noises that were assaulting my ear.

'What's this about a Blue-winged Teal?' he said. 'I've been there six times and not seen it. It doesn't exist! Where is it? In the reed bed? You stay there until I get there! Who else has seen it? Whose woman's voice is that I can hear? You tell her to stay there! I know a way into those reeds; I'll go in and flush it out. I've spent a fortune in petrol trying to find that bird. I'm telling you it doesn't exist!'

Phew! I stood there and listened to the tirade until I had had enough and simply said: 'I don't care what you think any more, I'm going home.' Without even a 'Goodbye', I terminated the call and left, safe in the knowledge that here was a friendship best forgotten. Recognition of such unbridled arrogance was okay but it did little for my blood pressure, and I wished that honour could have been satisfied in the old fashioned way. I remain to this day unsatisfied but, at least, civilized. This was the last but one conversation I would ever have with my erstwhile pal.

Call me a big kid if you want (I'm not alone, anyway) but setting sail for the Isles of Scilly in October bathes me in excitement. Of course, this year was special and I hoped to gather many ticks for my year list. It was rumoured that Lee was not going to the Islands this year. I have since learned that such myths are created from within when a rival has been identified. I knew for a fact that he would arrive after me and I hoped with all fervour that I would 'clean up' prior to his coming and the birds would henceforth have left.

I'm not sure what constitutes a 'flock', but if it is three, then we were fortunate enough to see a flock of Grey Phalaropes from *The Scillonian*. This was a great 'fillip for Philip', who had never seen the species before. Most of what we saw on that journey was new to Stuart, as he was not what one might call a 'birder'. He had an interest in natural history, although was seemingly more intrigued by the idea of 'hunting'. As a 'squaddie', who had served Queen and Country in Bosnia, Sierra Leone and God knows where else, where people gladly killed each other, he craved the quiet contemplation of watching his feathered friends. Of course, he was also aware of the political situation involving Lee and myself and, as a soldier, he found the darker side of human nature therein rather intriguing.

By its usual standards, the islands produced little of ornithological excitement in 2002, but, as usual, there was enough going on to suggest the prospect of greater glories. In all I came away with six additions to my year list, two of which were altogether new to me. One of these had been something of an embarrassment for several years, as every one else I had spoken to seemed to have seen at least one Rustic Bunting. However, my first sighting of the species was a source of great joy, and Gary took some excellent photographs of the bird that showed just how beautiful it was. Minor rarities included two Yellow-browed Warblers, a very coy Richard's Pipit and a Citrine Wagtail, but the highlight came on the 6th in Tresco.

At 3.35 p.m., Richard, Phil, Stuart and I were making our way back to the quay and the boat that would return us to St Mary's after a moderately successful and very enjoyable day's birding in Tresco. As we approached the sluice gate near Abbey Farm Cottage, I noticed a *Locustella* warbler perched openly on a sallow bush. The bird had a very obvious rufous-coloured rump and a primrose wash to the throat. The bill was strong and dagger-like and the 'mean' expression of the face was accentuated by a bold pale supercilium. I knew immediately that we were in the presence of something very special and said to my friends, 'That looks like a Pallas's Grasshopper Warbler!' Over the next hour or so we saw the bird several times and at one point it passed within about a metre of Stuart's face. All of us saw the salient features and, back at our rented flat that evening, made extensive notes and sketches. Afterwards, we voted on its identity. All agreed that the bird was indeed a Pallas 'gropper'.

Chapter 9

The next problem was what to do with the record. Had it been a 'normal' year, I would have been delighted to call out the record at the evening log – more especially as three other observers saw it – but this was no ordinary year and I could already hear the calls of 'Stringer' echoing through the Scillonian Club. We agreed that politically it would be best merely to call it a *Locustella* sp., as seen by four people, and thereafter furnish any interested parties with all the information regarding the sighting. Of course, a formal account would later be sent to the relevant authorities. I forget how many people asked us about the bird that evening. It was quite a few, and I believe many went to Tresco the following morning in search of it. We decided not to join them as we had all had fairly good views of it, and the idea of participating in the kind of scrimmage that took place in search of the same species on Blakeney Point the previous year did not appeal. Apart from in our dreams that night, it was never seen again.

The news of Lee's arrival in the islands enveloped me like the smoke from a cheap cigarette and my demeanour changed for the worse. I hate confrontation but will never back down from it: I would simply rather it avoided me. In hindsight, I see that this attitude is naive. If one is going to put oneself in this sort of situation, one had better expect the proverbial to hit the fan at some stage. The best policy is to face it head on – not try to avoid it, as this is impossible. By this point though, I was so angry with the man that I simply detested all that he stood for. I wanted to see the year through, beat him and deal with my feelings towards him at some future time when tempers were less strained. The Isles of Scilly are a very small place in which to have two aggrieved people, and the bad atmosphere that prevailed was clear for everyone to see. On two separate occasions, people I had never before met came up to me, shook my hand and said how much they supported my challenge to beat Lee. I was pleasantly surprised by this show of support for me. The former friend who I had defended previously from such vitriol was clearly not popular in all quarters. Realizing this made me feel better as I now knew that I had a great deal of backing. Perversely though, it was obvious that the support was not for me in particular but for anyone who tried to bring Lee down a peg or two. My flagging ego milked the encouragement for all that it was worth. The backhanded comments and pointing fingers from Lee's supporters at the evening logs hurt less now. I understood they came either from sycophants or bigots who had no desire to understand both sides of the story and who found it comforting to bathe in the reflected glory of being seen with this 'legendary' birder. Feeling less intimidated, I set off on the 10th to Tresco in search of a very elusive Short-toed Lark.

The whole day was spent around Castle Down where I laboured across the moorland in search of the lark. A couple of other birders were there early on but did not persevere for long and gave up after an hour or so. After having some lunch at the edge of the sea, I returned to the small flocks of Meadow Pipits and Skylarks with which my quarry was supposed to mingle. Almost at the point of giving up, a huge flock of pipits arrived from nowhere and amongst them was the Short-toed Lark. I was absolutely delighted to ring the bird in to RBA as I thought Lee was on a different island. He would therefore not be able to get to Tresco in time that day to see the bird – a species I knew he had not seen so far that year. As I left Castle Down I was infuriated to see him walking towards me. Worse, he even had the gall to ask me about the lark. I tried unsuccessfully to be civil and walked on angrily and in the knowledge that from now on, reluctantly, I would not be notifying RBA of any important birds that I saw. Later I was to speak with Dick Filby, who runs the service, and explain the change in my behaviour. I was delighted at how calmly he listened and sadly accepted the situation.

Lee missed the Short-toed Lark, as most of the pipits had left by the time he arrived at the site. He accosted Gary later in

Chapter 9

the afternoon and was disappointed in the response he got to his accusations that I had 'strung' the bird. At that evening's log, he reported 50 Meadow Pipits; smugly, I amended the figure to 120-plus. A few people laughed. On the mainland, a Western Bonelli's Warbler sniggered at me from Nanquidno Valley, Cornwall, and Pallas's and Radde's Warblers were positively in hysterics in Holkham Woods, just a few minutes from where I live.

Nothing new was seemingly arriving in the Scillies, and the weather suggested the situation would not change. However, some very promising winds were blowing onto the east coast, and, as Stuart and Phil were happy at the prospect of spending a week in Norfolk, we decided to leave the south-west early in the hope of seeing at least a couple of those warblers. We told no one of our plans in the hope that Lee would not find out and, like thieves in the night, we skulked away. Unfortunately, the Bonelli's Warbler had the same idea; to my annoyance, the Pallas's Warbler joined him; to my immense relief the Radde's Warbler hung on longer and its name ended up on my list; to my dismay a Black-throated Thrush and an Isabelline Shrike decided to spend a holiday in the Isles of Scilly. Mentally I felt mangled and I could sense bad tactical decisions lurking in the shadows like demons. I needed a rest but had now made the decision to go for anything and everything new that arrived. Rest was a luxury I could not afford. Within a week I was on the trail of a 'Mega' at Flamborough Head in Yorkshire.

On the evening of the 22nd, I found myself sitting bemusedly at home surrounded by my 'scope, bin's, rucksack, etc. At the time, I should have been in Yorkshire excitedly approaching my first ever look at a White-throated Sparrow. Instead, the person who should have been driving us there had just dropped me off outside my door and was heading happily homewards. That afternoon, we arranged to meet in Sculthorpe, and he had decided to drive as he did not like the smell of cigars

October – the Scilly season

in *The Enterprise*. Fair enough. However, it took him almost half an hour of soul-searching contemplation during which every possible permutation of smoke inhalation from car upholstery and clothes, deprivation of drugs and its likely effect on human demeanour during a long journey, fuel economy, driver experience and ability, proposed stopping places for food and bladder relief, as well as the probability of the bird remaining long enough for us to see it, were considered. He was thinking himself into a whirlpool of indecision and, at several points in his ruminations, elected not to go but then changed his mind. Finally, he decided to go, provided that he could drive, provided that…. The realization that I was not going to enjoy this journey was immediate. Within twenty minutes he needed to stop to go to the loo and, as he did so, I sat in the car watching the time pass by.

I worked out in my mind that, had I not arranged to go with this chap, I would already have been well past Peterborough and on the northbound A17, heading towards the A1 and certain glory. The pager relayed news of no recent sighting of the sparrow. By the time his bladder was emptied, 'The Thinking Man' had had time to become worried about our route and it was necessary to discuss it further. The minutes ticked away as I tried to convince him that I knew the way. By now, I was desperate to get properly under way and I insisted that we got going. A short, uncomfortable silence descended as the car moved off. Perhaps this would be the end of all the procrastination and we could set to the job in hand.

'Still no further sign…,' said the pager.

'I really should pick up something to eat,' said The Thinking Man.

My heart sank. He was now very concerned about the lack of sparrow sightings and was also cultivating a considerable hunger. Ominously, we were approaching the services near Peterborough where at least one of these problems could be

Chapter 9

addressed and, sure enough, the statement I had been dreading was soon booming around the car.

'I'll tell you what, let's stop at the services and have a coffee and a bite to eat and see what news the pager brings while we are doing so!' Off he strolled towards his burger and coffee and I stayed with the car, smoking for England.

Over two hours had elapsed since our meeting. When he returned to the car he was wearing a very serious expression. I knew instinctively what was coming and was not surprised to hear his authoritative observation that the bird had obviously gone and that there was consequently no point in continuing our journey. There was certainly no point in trying to discuss the matter, as his mind was well and truly made up. As he dropped me off at home he was full of well-meaning advice on how I should go about seeing the bird the following day, on birding in general and twitching in particular. Sadly, he had commitments tomorrow and would not be able to join me.

I walked into the house dazed, and it took me several minutes to compute the events of the last few hours. When I had done so I phoned Nessie in a rage. For a few moments we competed for the title 'Best Adjective to Describe Someone That Has Just Upset You, 2002'. I think Nessie may have just shaded it despite my very strong late challenge on hearing the news of a further sighting of the sparrow. I was able later to regain the title when describing the Leeds United chairman's decision to sell Jonathan Woodgate to Newcastle – despite his assurances to the then manager Terry Venables that he would do no such thing. The crumbling of the Leeds Empire continued.

At some ungodly hour that night I set off alone for Flamborough and the following morning, despite a long, cold wait, I saw the White-throated Sparrow. I did not know how it managed to get all the way from North America and I did not care. Ship-assisted or not, it was my favourite bird of the year. A 'cracking' bird, as they say, giving 'crippling' views. Someone, whose name I'm afraid I don't remember, shook my hand and hoped that I would beat Lee, and all seemed well with the world. To add to my joy, a little bunting was available at Atwick, a minor diversion on my way back to Norfolk.

Over the course of the year, an enigmatic 'Orange-billed Tern' had appeared now and again, and I had tried for it twice and failed. Some thought it was a Lesser-crested Tern and some, an Elegant Tern. The consensus was ever swinging towards the latter, and I was desperately disappointed to have missed it. Then, to my amazement, a further opportunity presented itself. The only problem was that it was in the west of Ireland. Fortunately, two other people were interested in going and so ensued the craziest adventure of the year.

The ferry from Fishguard sailed at around 3.00 a.m. and I was accompanied by James Hanlon and Paul Holmes. The weather was abominable and the crossing extremely rough. The corridors, lounges and toilets were reminiscent of a post-apocalyptic bunker. A very worried lady approached me as I left the loo on one occasion and asked if there was a small boy therein.

'Madam,' I said, 'There are many small boys in there. Most of them are green,' was my Churchillian reply.

To offer sympathy to the unfortunate sufferers of this wretched malaise is futile, as they merely crave Garbo-like solitude. I therefore decided that the best course of action was to ignore them and head for the bar. There I drank a few pints of grotesque lager and snoozed intermittently. Several people fell heavily from their seats, and I was gracious enough to put it down to the bucking and rolling of the ship.

Paul and James slept through most of the journey and were in good health when we finally arrived at Rosslare. We had booked a day-return ticket which meant that we had to get to Dingle Bay and back for the evening ferry – a round journey of over 400 miles. It was not going to be easy, and we calculated that we would probably have less than an hour to find the bird on reaching the site. To make matters even more pressing, a second target, in the form of a Forster's Tern, was also believed to be in the area.

By the time we reached Dingle, the weather had worsened and our weary spirits were drenched at the hands of a continuous downpour. Paul scanned one area of the harbour and James and I another. Miraculously, I quickly located the Elegant Tern, though Paul was more difficult to find. Eventually I tracked him down and we were all able to enjoy the bird. We were almost fooled by a strange-looking Sandwich Tern that did a wonderful impersonation of our second quarry. But common sense prevailed, and we left on our return drive with (as I felt) only half the mission accomplished. How ungrateful can you get?

I comforted myself in the improbable thought that perhaps there never was a Forster's tern there, and that our little friend had been more successful in duping some other unfortunate birder. Time was passing swiftly by and, seemingly impossibly, the weather was deteriorating further.

By the halfway point of our return journey across Ireland the night had closed in, the wind had reached at least gale force and the rain had become torrential and unceasing. I had never driven so hard in such treacherous conditions. At every bend *The Enterprise*'s hold on the road failed and her stern fishtailed. The many patches of wet leaves compounded the situation, but on we pushed. Visibility through the windscreen was down to perhaps twenty yards and even then it was sporadic, as the wipers simply could not cope with the huge quantities of water being thrown at them. At the back of our minds was the nagging doubt that the ferry would not be able to sail in such conditions. Yet it was imperative to get back to Rosslare – just in case.

In the tempest ahead of *The Enterprise* we spotted an array of lights that obviously belonged to some form of vehicle but could not work out what it was. One thing for sure, it was going like a 'bat out of Hell', and I had difficulty keeping up with it. Some of the lights appeared to bounce up and down in alarming fashion. We decided that it must be a car pulling some sort of trailer. During the briefest of lapses in the deluge we saw to our immense amusement that it was indeed a trailer and on its back was ... a boat! Perhaps, like Noah, the owner had inside information on the severity of the storm and was preparing for the worse. Perhaps he was in search of some of his favourite animals – two by two.

As we drew within twenty miles of Rosslare, Paul phoned the ferry company and was told that the ship would have one chance only to leave port and we had therefore to arrive slightly earlier than originally arranged. We were probably not going to make it.

The quality of the roads on approaching Rosslare is a big improvement on the ones we had been used to further west, and I felt able to push on even harder – despite aquaplaning every now and then. Overtaking opportunities were also more frequent, and I determined to give it my very best shot. All thoughts of fatigue disappeared. I imagined myself in the cockpit of a Formula One racing car with the name 'Schumacher' painted stylishly along the front wing. Higher and higher went the speedometer as I passed several vehicles with consummate ease. Unfortunately, one of them was a police car and its occupant was less than amused. His flashing blue light appeared in my rear-view mirror; I knew that I was 'nicked'. Worse still was the realization that, however short the delay in processing my misdemeanour, we were now definitely not going to make the ferry.

As I got out of *The Enterprise* I glanced up at the policeman and noticed the look of unadulterated fury on his face. He showed me the reading on his radar gun and informed me that it was taken before I started overtaking anyone. I was as contrite as it is possible to be under the circumstances. This seemed to calm

Chapter 9

him slightly. I explained that we had to get Paul home for the following day, as he was a teacher and had exams to supervise in the morning. True as it kind of was, this irritated the policeman. I'm sure he had heard every excuse in the book and probably felt I should have done a lot better. I decided that further excuses were inadvisable and returned to the trusted contriteness. He went back to his car with my licence in hand; thoughts of my drink-driving conviction of some six years ago welled over me.

I knew that I would pass a breath test because, since that conviction, I have been extremely careful about repeating that particular mistake, but further delays could well follow. Fortunately they didn't. Now on first name terms he said, 'Adrian, I'm afraid I'm going to have to do you!' He then gave me the statutory fine for the offence and sent us on our way. I am sure that, had I been anything less than humble, he could well have thrown the book at me. I was further grateful that, having committed the offence in a 'foreign' country, no further points would be added to my somewhat crowded licence. I was ordered to pay 60 Euros, and my partners in crime immediately offered to pay a third each. I had escaped lightly for driving recklessly and dangerously and shall always remember that kind policeman and his sense of fair play. We missed the ferry.

We had no money, Paul needed to be in Ipswich by the next morning, our mobiles would not work, the weather was forecast to deteriorate even further and we all needed a pint or two. The landlord of a chosen pub saw us coming and offered to supply us with the latter, provided we paid 'one for one' pounds sterling to Euro. This was obviously a rip-off at which he was clearly an expert. He had surely experienced the predicament before and knew that we had no choice but to accept. Reluctantly we did so and, after the first couple of drinks, resigned ourselves to defeat and enjoyed the beer.

Without Euros we would not be able to stay in a B&B, at least not for a sensible price. We decided that we would sleep in

October – the Scilly season

the car. We were getting a few Euros in change that would allow us to phone our loved ones and other important people with the briefest of messages. Slowly we were getting sozzled which, in my experience, frees one's thought processes and allows one to make unhasty decisions. We were stuck and that was that: we would have to make the best of it.

After a few beers we retired to *The Enterprise* where we covered ourselves in whatever coats and other warm materials we could find and slept surprisingly well, more especially considering the car rocked mercilessly through the night in the ever-increasing wind. No one snored, no one talked in their sleep, and the following morning we awoke refreshed, if dishevelled.

The day was a new one, and we would make the most of it. The first priority, of course, was a bank. This we found, and the necessary funds were extracted to pay the speeding ticket and buy the largest breakfast in Christendom. After filling the coffers of the local constabulary and our bellies, we decided to spend the day birding and simply hope that the ferry would sail that evening. There was a further report of a Forster's Tern close to where we were and consequently we felt that our luck was changing. In respect of the tern, it did not, but we saw about 60 bird species that day, and the more relaxed atmosphere in the face of resignation meant that we had a lot of fun. I am not sure whether Paul realizes it (though I suspect he does) but his voice, and sometimes his vocal inflection, is very similar to Rowan Atkinson's character Black Adder.

We were thinking about where to get lunch. We were despicable, if not frightening, in appearance, probably quite smelly, and the only sign of civilization in view was a domesticated cow. In answer to James's query on the subject, Paul replied, 'Well, I thought a French bistro. Boeuf Bourguignon, perhaps, and some fine wines.' I laughed until my sides hurt. James and I had an alternative cunning plan whereby we could try 'The Local Shop', however, for some reason, unlike any such establishment in England, pies, pasties, sausage rolls, Scotch eggs and other 'birding fare' were unavailable. Paul informed us with great authority that any country so closely allied with litigation-conscious mainland Europe would not be allowed to sell such rubbish to its citizens. Dishevelled and dispirited, I ate something healthy, but so bland was it I don't remember what it was. I think it contained pasta.

Through the day the weather improved and we became more and more confident that our ship would sail that evening. Our day ended with a search for food at several pubs around Rosslare. For people of frugal tastes such a task should not be difficult, but our Irish cousins made it so.

Having tried several establishments, each of which offered meals that were overly priced, we came across a pub with such simple pleasures as pie and chips, lasagne and chips, fish and chips, in fact, anything and chips. Rubbing our hands in anticipation, we placed our order whereupon the young lady behind the bar disappeared for a while. On returning, she informed us that we could not have the meals that we wanted because there was only one potato left. Despite the fact that every single meal on the menu included chips, she stood in gallant anticipation, pencil poised above notepad, waiting for our alternative choice of dish. In disbelief, we left and decided that partial starvation would be less punishing than trying elsewhere. However, by good fortune, we passed a sort of chip shop where the omens looked good for the continued existence of potatoes. To our delight, we discovered that the second great Irish potato famine was over and so ordered our meals. Mine was utterly disgusting and most of it ended up in a waste bin that was conveniently placed close to the shop. I think Paul and James were so hungry that they could not resist the slop put in front of them, but the noises, which accompanied their meals, were not ones of satisfaction.

On arrival at the ferry terminal we were assured the ship would indeed sail that evening. With great relief we looked at each other and smiled. The atmosphere amongst us changed from one of resigned good humour to genuine anticipation of completing our mission. Paul and James decided to seek out the coffee lounge and I elected to sit in the car and take a nap. Before I knew it, the queue in which *The Enterprise* was standing was beginning to move. For some reason, the authorities were processing the passengers early and I was being ushered to the check-in without my companions. When I got to the point of no return I explained the situation to the man in charge. I fully expected him to say, 'Hard luck, mate. Either get on now or push off!' Instead he waved me dismissively across several lines of oncoming articulated lorries and told me to wait. Taking my life in my hands, I did as ordered and then wondered what on earth I was supposed to do. To their credit, Paul and James had 'sussed' the situation and somehow managed to find me, though the latter somewhat worryingly later than the former. Finally we were reunited and were the last people to board. By comparison with what had gone before, the journey home was without incident.

Paul got to school on time; alas, I have never seen him since. James placated his worried mother who had not been able to contact him whilst he was in Ireland and we have since become very good friends. Returning through Thetford Forest made me feel close to home, and the following day *The Enterprise* sat with all her doors open to the fresh air in an attempt to regain the odours of civilisation. The day after that I was off again on the continuing quest to find strange new worlds of experience. A Grey-cheeked Thrush had flown across the Atlantic Ocean and had landed in the Isles of Scilly. Here we go again.

The usual early start from Sculthorpe was to no avail on this occasion, as the weather was so grim that there were no flights from the mainland and there were no sailings available on *The*

Scillonian. However, the Western Bonelli's Warbler was still at Land's End, and I was able to get reasonable views through the worsening fog before seeking solace at a pub in St Just. The following morning was greeted by better weather and with an air of terrific excitement and anticipation.

I boarded *The Scillonian* with a handful of other birders, some of whom I had shared the frustrations of the previous day's lack of transport. At roughly the halfway point of the crossing, we learned with great delight, and relief, that the thrush was still in residence. It was then that someone came over to chat to me. I recognised him as Les Holliwell, the third person present on my very first birding trip with Lee. I had seen him around and about on several occasions since, but never to speak to. The conversation inevitably turned to year-listings, and it soon became apparent that he and Lee had suffered a major 'falling-out'.

He did not recognize me from that trip some two and a half years ago. I was quietly amused when he asked if I knew who '… this bloke Adrian Riley is?' Impishly I said that I did and that he seemed an okay sort of chap.

'How well do you know him? No one else has heard of him before.'

'Oh, pretty well,' I said.

'Well, who is he? What does he look like?'

I couldn't keep a straight face any longer and said, 'He looks like me.'

The dawning of recognition on Les's face was a joy to behold and we both laughed like drains. From that moment on we chatted incessantly about the year I was having and the problems I was likely to encounter having dared to challenge Lee for his title.

He introduced me to Adrian Webb who claimed (rightly in my opinion) the all-time year-list record in 2000 and incurred the most awful wrath from Lee, some of which spilled over to national television and a national broadsheet. At the time I viewed the ensuing war with great hilarity, as the general public were served with just the fuel to kindle its suspicions about the sanity of birdwatchers. I vowed I would never allow myself to be drawn into such a farce. Again, how naive can one get.

Les, Adrian and Adrian's father, Dave, re-taught me on that trip that birding can be fun. It had been no such thing for many a month, and I thought that the battle with Lee had probably ruined my hobby for good. Instead, the laughs we had that day and the encouragement I was given to actually go for Adrian's record were a wonderful tonic. This probably saved me from the self-devouring monster of bitterness, revenge and cynicism. To make things even better, we all saw the Grey-cheeked Thrush and were treated to the added bonus of a Blyth's Reed Warbler at the old churchyard in St Mary's.

The day was indeed complete, and I drove home having reached the end of October a happy man. Had it not been for Les, Adrian and Dave, I would merely have been successful, and where's the fun in that? My total was now on 370, but only a handful of people knew, and my news blackout was from now on to include the Surfbirds league table. I would keep that man guessing until it drove him crazy.

On my return, Jason phoned me with the news that Lee, on his website, had disqualified me from his tabulations [sic] for '... persistently fabricating sightings from Shetland to Devon.' Why he did not extend his range further south-west to where I allegedly 'strung' the Short-toed Lark in Tresco, I cannot imagine. Of course, I was furious but, at the same time, was strangely relieved. I no longer had to take Lee seriously, as he was satisfyingly in danger of hoisting himself by his own petard by repeating his risible attempts at publicly discrediting his opponents (see Stephen Moss, *The Guardian*, April, 2001). Further, his actions seemed like those of someone who was feeling threatened by a person who he took very seriously indeed.

Chapter 9

I took my reputation, not as a birder but as a scientist and professional Lepidoptera recorder, seriously enough to seek legal advice on how to remove his possibly libellous comments from the public domain. Seventy pounds sterling in legal fees bought me the advice I could have got for nothing in the local pub. Seemingly there was not much I could do, as the comments, libellous though they may have appeared to be, were on Lee's own website and were therefore not actually in the aforementioned public domain. I could have done without losing seventy quid but, if needs be, I could threaten the man with legal action with a clear conscience should I wish to do so, as it was now a real option (though it would be expensive and probably ultimately fruitless).

In the meantime Jason, Phil, Richard, Alex and Peter Thomas were concocting a letter to *Birdwatch* magazine expressing their disgust at such repeatedly defamatory behaviour and comments in the face of possible defeat. I had many phone calls of support and fervent best wishes in my quest to win the competition. Lee may have continued to make decisions concerning the integrity of fellow competitors within his following, but it appears that there were ever fewer people who were prepared to listen to him. I decided that my best course of action would be to carry on smiling, exceed his total for the year and let others judge who the winner was.

November and December – the final furlong

Her Majesty the Queen had completed a wonderful tour of the British Isles in celebration of her golden jubilee – a testament to her stamina after many an *'annus horribilis'*. England's cricketers had performed admirably in two Test series against Sri Lanka (a 2-0 win) and India (a 1-1 draw, despite the brilliance of Sachin Tendulkar and Rahul Dravid). Our footballers gave (almost) their all in an extremely entertaining World Cup competition during which the flamboyant and much evolved techniques of the Far Eastern countries enthralled all but the purists. England progressed to the semi-finals but was dumped by the eventual winners, Brazil, despite taking the lead through a Michael Owen goal. This competition saw the beginning of the end for one of our greatest sporting servants, David Seaman, the England goalkeeper who has since handed over the keeper's jersey. Tim Henman also made a semi-final but failed to play tennis at a level that would surely have drawn Queen Elizabeth to the final amidst deafening cheers from Wimbledon Centre Court and Henman Hill. Paula Radcliff blazed an invincible trail in various long-distance running events and England's Rugby Union team was growing into a side that would soon become the envy of the world. Arsenal looked the most likely to succeed in the Premier League, whereas Manchester United seemed uncharacteristically out of touch. The Leeds Empire continued to crumble since Terry Venables' appointment as manager appeared to be ever more a publicity stunt than a realistic option for the future. Relegation was the naughty word echoing around Elland Road. Lennox Lewis remained Heavyweight Champion of the World after defeating old ear-biter 'Iron' Mike Tyson and Lee was to date the current UK Twitcher of the Year. But it was still only November, and much could yet change.

The only thing that remained constant was Leeds' inescapable slide into a relegation battle – one which, if they lost, could without doubt threaten the very existence of the club. As we moved into winter, so our cricketers flew south to Australia where, I am afraid to say, they were brought down to earth with an almighty bump. Henman evaporated into the ether of the world circuit, whence little drama escapes. Meanwhile, Lewis disappeared for the heavyweight boxer's obligatory months of inactivity during which the money men do their utmost to make themselves look absurd. One other thing was changing – it wasn't just Leeds United that was courting disaster – Lee's United was also in big, big trouble.

According to his website, on the 29th of October, he was on 359 birds whilst at the very end of October, I was on 370. He was perhaps guessing at my tally as he often does so with fellow competitors. Many entries on his UK400 tables are incorrect. In fact, Jason ended up with some fifteen more birds during 2000 than he actually saw; several other birders have told me similar tales. If he was indeed guessing, then his estimations were way off target. Perhaps, having dismissed his opponent, he felt secure enough to make public his total and hope that, ashamed and ridiculed, I would simply run away with my tail between my legs. Either way, I no longer cared and was satisfied that, provided I now saw everything that became available, I would beat him. Remember, he claimed to have seen 221 species during January. That meant there were precious few, if any, winter birds left to get during the latter part of the year. Hence, there could not possibly now be enough twitches during the last two months for him to catch up, as he would need no less than 11 in the relatively lean last two months of the year. Neither of us could have imagined though, what an incredible end the year would bring in terms of rare birds. I certainly could not have imagined just how low a competitor could stoop in an attempt to prevent his rival getting to a twitch.

On the 1st of November, a very obliging Dusky Warbler in Suffolk became my first addition along the home straight. Whilst Alex and I watched the bird, our enjoyment was spoilt by the news that Lee was on his way. Although this later proved unfounded, we left anyway. The following day we travelled to Hengistbury Head in Dorset for a very serious-looking Bobolink that had strayed across the Atlantic from North America. There, Jason and I met Phil and we had great pleasure watching the bird until Jason and I went on to West Lulworth for a Pallas's Warbler. Unfortunately, the warbler had flown on, and I was beginning to think that I would not see this reasonably regular visitor during my 'big year'. The drive home that day was one of the worst I can remember, with the rain simply lashing down and our contact with the road becoming at best tenuous. Then, on the 7th came the most extraordinary day of the whole venture. I shall quote directly from my diary. When put in writing it may not seem much, but I suggest you try it.

Nov. 7th, 2004

'Left home for Penzance at around midnight. A killdeer and a paddyfield warbler have arrived in St Agnes, Scilly. Simply got to see these birds and must get the first flight out. Probably a two-day job. Helicopter got me to St Mary's about 9.00 a.m. and [I] caught the bus to the Quay. Enough space aboard a speedboat for me and a newly found mate and we just caught it in time. Thrashed across to St Agnes and got soaked to the skin as I didn't put my waterproofs on – bloody idiot. Hamlet cigars still dry, thank God. Lit one on arrival and rushed to the bird – what a cracker. Searched frozen and sodden for ages for the paddyfield warbler but it seemed to have left. Heard that Lee had seen it the previous day – f*** it! Hung around shivering waiting for a boat to take me back to St Mary's. Seriously cold now – reminds me of Foula. Standard boat gets me back without further drenching and got the bus back to the airport. Chopper flight on time and soon back in Penzance. Very relieved to get into *The Enterprise* and get the heating on full blast. Hacked it back to Sculthorpe and at 10.50 p.m. standing at the bar of The Horse and Groom with a pint in my hand. Still have a wet crotch from the speedboat crossing at 9.30 this morning. Bloody chuffed, though. Well done, Ade!'

On the following day, I scoured the bleak and muddy fens of Cambridgeshire for the fourth time in search of an American Golden Plover. On a previous attempt I had seen a Golden Plover with a bright supercilium and had wondered if someone had made a serious mistake. A friendly farmer stopped for a chat. I explained that the bird had apparently been seen that morning. However, the huge flock of plovers had been disturbed and had moved far out of view to a distant field. As luck would have it, the track, which led pretty well directly to the birds, belonged to the farmer, and he very kindly gave me permission to drive along it in order to scan the birds. He stayed with me for a while, and I was very pleased to be able to show him the reason for all the fuss. I believe this was the last time the bird was seen.

My journeys to the fens were extremely dirty, as the tracks were thick with a glutinous mud that seemed to stick to everything. After one visit, Alex and I popped into Wells-next-the-Sea, Norfolk, where I waited in *The Enterprise* while he searched for a pasty. Two young girls were walking along the road towards me and when they saw the state of my car, their faces turned to expressions of complete disgust. I was rather proud of this achievement but, on relating the story to Nessie, I was immediately ordered outside, armed with bucket and sponge. It was then that I affirmed my belief that the opposite sex does not reason with logic. Had Nessie done so she would have realized that the cleaning exercise was futile, as I had to go back to the fens anyway. Her response to this argument was swift and incisive and involved many expletives surrounding the words 'lazy', 'idle', etc.

For about 24 hours *The Enterprise* looked wonderful; however, I made sure I was absent when Nessie returned from work the following day. If the car is parked at home but I am not, then it is a fair bet that I will be in the pub struggling with the *Daily Telegraph* crossword. Nessie knows this only too well, yet the walk from home to The Horse and Groom is usually just long enough to take the edge off her grievances. It is when she doesn't show at the expected time of verbal execution that one needs to worry. One across: Ring small simpleton and strike. --, ----.

This was a period during which the weather was conducive to sea-watching, and I had spent several early morning sessions at Cley in search of the many Little Auks that were being reported off our coasts. On the 9th, I was successful and was delighted to share that success with a lady who had been trying for many hours to find one. She had never seen the species before and was thrilled when I showed it to her. I think I got more joy out of seeing the expression on her face than in finding the auk. When I stop feeling this way I shall give up birding altogether. Incidentally, I learned recently that during his monumental year in 2000, when Adrian Webb broke the year-listing record, he did not see a Little Auk. These diminutive blighters can surely be elusive.

After a short lull, a Red-flanked Bluetail visited Gibraltar Point in Lincolnshire. I was fortunate enough to see the bird on the 16th and enjoyed every minute of that sweet creature – especially as it was a species Lee had already seen but I had missed. As I left, several people were talking about Lee in a less than complimentary way, and John Pegden gave a pleasant, if rather weary wave and smile. I believe he missed most of the early autumn migration through commitments at work and I wondered if he had perhaps already resigned himself to defeat. I felt a certain sympathy. His achievements in 2002 were extraordinary, considering he was also working full-time. In fact, I think they more or less outshine both Lee's and mine as we had the time to chase birds wherever and whenever we wanted.

November closed with another 'catch-up' bird. Lee had already seen a Forster's Tern, and I had to wait until the 27th to claw it back. I was particularly pleased with this bird because Paul, James and I had worked hard, long and ultimately unsuccessfully for it during our trip to Ireland. The weather in Cornwall that day was horrendous, and the sight of a poor bedraggled fellow birder, pushing his way through the torrential rain, forced me by sheer pity to break news silence. I felt so sorry for that poor man that I wanted to give him as much encouragement as possible. I just hope he was carrying a pager. Luckily for me I didn't even have to get out of the car, as the tern flew obligingly and elegantly right in front of the pub car park.

Thus ended November, and I felt confident that, with my total now on 377, things were really going my way. Not only had I seen every new bird available but had also connected with birds which Lee had already seen. There was surely no way he now could catch me since I expected few new birds to arrive during December. However, the drama was not quite over yet.

A veritable thorn in my flesh in the shape of a Pallas's Warbler had taken residence in St Mary's. It was a long way to go for such a bird: it was hardly a 'Mega'. One thing, though, was for sure. There would not be another one this year. The reader may by now have gathered that I enjoy a glass or two of the 'amber nectar' and so you might imagine what my birthdays are usually like. However, the celebrations would have to be put on hold this year, as on the 3rd I set off once again for the Isles of Scilly.

What a lovely birthday present I was to get. Not only was my primary target still at Lower Moors, but also no fewer than three Firecrests and a Yellow-browed Warbler were there also. As a late morning drizzle began to fall and the air became moist and surprisingly heavy for December, all the warblers, including many Chiffchaffs and the odd Blackcap and Goldcrest, fed openly by darting from the sallow bushes like flycatchers. It was a magical sight and one that I feasted on for maybe an hour before the drizzle turned to rain and my feathered friends sought cover in the dense scrub. I ran for one of the hides. There I sat in silence as a pair of Mallards preened themselves in satisfied style, no doubt enjoying the solitude, which is so rare here during the height of the birding season. Stupidly, I blew some cigar smoke through the window. Startled, the ducks realized they were not alone and flew noisily away. As quiet again settled over the pond, I felt a wave of emotion wash over me as I remembered the wonderful times I had spent here with Nessie and the pals gained along the way. What an exquisitely lonely place this was without their laughter. Sadly I left it to the ghosts of birders past and looked forward to my next visit when, hopefully, I would be without the pressure of competitive twitching.

I did not want to return this year and, fortunately, I did not have to. I walked slowly to the airfield and got very wet indeed. As I arrived I met Bob Flood and we chatted in lively fashion about the wonderful end to the year it had been for the islands. The conversation inevitably turned to Lee, and Bob expressed his concern about the Wilson's Storm-petrel and Cory's Shearwaters that Lee had claimed earlier in the year. Bob said in no uncertain terms that these records could not be accepted or counted – a view with which I agreed. I added that it was probably irrelevant anyway, because Lee was unlikely to send in an official report of his sightings. Bob nodded sagely. He then told me something which beggared belief.

Lee had been in the islands on the 6th of November to see the Killdeer and the Paddyfield Warbler. Having seen the former and presumably satisfied himself that I had not, he phoned RBA and told them that the bird had been killed by a Peregrine. Whoever was on duty had the nous to chase the story up. He immediately rang Bob and asked him if it was true. It was not. The bird was alive and well. I suspected this might be an attempt to prevent other people from seeing the Killdeer. I was boiling with fury but solid in the knowledge that I had, in my own mind, won the title, no matter how many birds Lee went on to claim. On my way home, I learned that he had now published a tally of 374. This meant that he had to have seen fifteen new birds during November – a feat that I personally considered impossible but, if real, still meant that he was three birds behind me in the race. Despite my comments regarding having already won by default, I still would not be satisfied until we had published our final totals at the end of the year.

With this in mind, I made the ridiculously long journey to Orkney on the 6th for the Rufous Turtle Dove, Britain's first 'twitchable' specimen of this bird. Here Lee excelled himself by shouting sarcastic comments in my direction across the harbour at Stromness. Several people loosely in his company tried desperately to extract my total from me. However, all failed as I knew exactly where and how quickly that information would fly.

It was a thoroughly miserable day, made slightly less tense by a few games of pool and a couple of pints of beer with James. He and my travelling companions, Les and Adrian, cheered me up no end and helped me control my fraying temper. Richard Porter once said to me: 'Whatever you do, Adrian, maintain your dignity.' Those wise words went round and around in my mind; they kept my feet on the ground, my hands in my pockets and my mouth shut. The only satisfaction I gained from the day (the dove was, I'm afraid, inconsequential) was that during Lee's tirade, he shouted, '…there's the top Surfbirds man. 374 species – all substantiated records…'. He was wonderfully off the mark as my total was then on 379. I was told during the course of the day that Lee's total was now on 377. How on earth he could have seen three new birds in three days at this time escaped me, but his methods had supposedly put him only two behind. I didn't believe it for one minute, yet I still wanted to see those end-of-year totals – naturally with mine greater.

On Christmas Eve, I found myself in Oxfordshire, wondering how on earth a Baikal Teal could have found its way there and why this year in particular should produce such a glut of late rarities. The duck was probably as dodgy as Hell (i.e. an escapee from a wildlife fowl collection). I was by now becoming ever more aware of Lee's tactics and could almost hear his voice deriding the bird's credentials and urging me not to bother with it as he watched it through his 'scope. I was not in the mood for messing about and went for it anyway. Had I done the same with the Hooded Merganser, I would have enhanced my street credibility no end, but it's never too late to learn. Unfortunately, I had to break 'radio silence' again because I could not find the site. Dick Filby was most helpful, and eventually the bird was bagged.

Amongst all the emotion and chaos, Ian Burrows and I still found excuse enough to go to Warham Greens on Christmas morning to look for the Pallid Harrier that had roosted there the night before. We didn't see it but felt good for trying, and Nessie and I had a fantastic Christmas the following day. Still it was not the end. On the 29th of December, a Blyth's Pipit was found at Gringley Carr, Nottinghamshire. In by now habitual fashion, I was on the road early the following morning and soon found myself in contact with the bird. The farmer who owned the field in which the pipit resided had written on a sign the grim instructions to 'keep out', but, I am afraid to say, I along with several local birders ignored all warnings. Flushed with victory, I returned home in quiet confidence and the certain knowledge that, with only one day of the year left, nothing else could happen and that would be that. However, here I was again wrong.

Chapter 10

On the morning of New Year's Eve, the 'Mega' alert went off. A Black-browed Albatross had been seen off the Norfolk coast near Mundesley. I sat in my kitchen behind a cup of coffee and thought, 'F*** it! I can't be beaten now. If Lee claims he can get to Norfolk in time to see this bird, he truly is a hero and is welcome to it. I'm going to the pub.' And so ended my great adventure – just as it started – over a pint and another uncompleted crossword. Now there was the small matter of our totals. Mine was 381.

The nineteenth hole

The first thing I had to do was wait. I was determined not to publish my total until Lee had published his. Enough people knew how many birds I had seen and my score was now 'set in stone'. I did not really trust my rival and so was wary about revealing my hand first. The second thing I had to do was get rid of that Bufflehead, as its inclusion in my list was certain to cause embarrassment at some later date. My official total was therefore 380.

Just a few days after the turn of the year, I got an unexpected phone call from Jason who told me that Lee had announced on his website that he had seen 379 species in 2002. I was stunned; he had played straight into my hands. Jason gave me his congratulations and carried out my request to publish my total on Surfbirds as soon as possible. The game was over. I had won. I got very, very drunk.

The UK400 club proudly announced that once again great fun was had by all in the annual listing competition – the only blight being the unfortunate disqualification of one Norfolk birder for cheating. On hearing about this I saw red and did what I thought I would never do again. I turned my phone to 'Lee' and pressed 'call'. Nessie sat with me while we spoke, as I needed someone both to hear what was said and to give me a firm kick should I start to lose my calm. Many of the things that were said by Lee were regretful, sentimental and very personal and should, for the sake of discretion, remain private. Suffice to say, I found that conversation very uncomfortable. I don't think I have ever remained so collected whilst giving someone a tongue-lashing, and Lee was left in no doubts as to my opinion of his behaviour. I concluded by insisting that his comments be removed from his website and, to my astonishment and to his credit, they had gone by the following day. Unfortunately, the apology I asked for did not appear. Alex, Phil, Jason, Ian and Nessie persuaded me to write a book about the year, and I then decided to do so. Although I have published numerous scientific papers and three books on butterflies and moths, I had never undertaken a work of this type and was, not surprisingly, rather nervous about it.

Whilst all this was happening, *Birdwatch* magazine had been trying to find out who I was and how I could be contacted. Luckily someone there knew Les and he consequently passed on to me the Assistant Editor David Mairs' telephone number. Within a few days we were having an interview over the phone and the March issue 2003 (No. 129, pp 6-7) carried in its contents page the heading 'Have you heard? The trials and tribulations of Britain's new top year-lister…'. A two-page article appeared of which I am understandably proud, although I still look at it and think, 'Is this really me?'

For the record, a couple of things need to be put straight. Some thought I had gone a little softly on Lee in the article, but common sense has to prevail in such circumstances. There are libel laws, after all. Also, the title of 'Top Year-lister' is perhaps not quite accurate as many birders, such as Adrian, Les and Richard Bonser, achieve amazing totals *every* year. This takes the kind of determination and stamina which I fear I lack.

As I write these concluding sentences, July 2003 is coming to a close and I still have not really recovered. The appearance of the article was closely, and in hindsight predictably, followed by yet more defamatory remarks from the UK400 Club. Lee vehemently denied the incident at Stromness and decided in his wisdom that I had seen somewhere in the region of 350 species. An exact figure was quoted, but so astonished was I at his 'revised' total for me that I dismissed it and immediately consigned it to my mental 'recycle bin'. Interestingly, the comments were removed almost immediately. I have often wondered why.

There is no doubt in my mind that I won the competition fair and square, but would it perhaps be more accurate to say that Lee had lost? I think on reflection that it would. Firstly, the incident with the Killdeer, if my suspicions were correct, would warrant immediate disqualification under a properly policed system. Secondly, his claims of certain birds such as the Wilson's Storm-petrel and the Cory's Shearwater off Porthgwarra would never stand official scrutiny. Those particular birds were far too distant for accurate identification – a fact supported by others who were there at the time. The Cornish Ortolan Bunting is another example made particularly interesting by the fact that I found the bird but could not justify recording it as such, because views of it were inconclusive. These three instances well illustrate the human tendency to sometimes see what one wants to see. This is perfectly natural and we have all, at some time, fallen into this trap. However, the appointed (self- or otherwise) referee in a competition such as this should be beyond suspicion and reproach, especially if that person regularly and fiercely calls into doubt the integrity and honesty of his fellow competitors. Clearly, the three instances I have described suggest this is not the case at present. Thirdly, and leading on from the last point, I believe Lee has not submitted descriptions or records for scrutiny elsewhere. I am certain that none of the aforementioned three species records, for example, would be accepted by the British Birds Rarity Committee. All of my records of rarities were sent to the county recorders at the end of the year. Unwillingness to comply with such a fundamental requirement and abide by the decisions of an independent referee should result in disqualification under normal circumstances. Unfortunately, the present circumstances were anything but normal.

I advise anyone who wants to go for the annual title to do so quietly and privately or with a group of friends with whom they can have some fun. Keep your eyes on what your competitors are doing and keep your ongoing tally to yourself. Nevertheless, at the end of the year, make sure all your rarity descriptions are sent to the appropriate county recorders and do not make your final total public until your rivals' are known and, preferably, published either on the Internet or in the birding literature. There is little point in shouting victory from the rooftops as there is no prize, no money and a lot of negative publicity will certainly ensue. You will not find fame here – possibly only infamy. Furthermore, you may have to spend most of the following summer indoors, writing a book about it all.

I shall end with another direct quote from my diary.

'This is the end of an extraordinary year. I have won the year-list race with 380 bird species. My nearest rival is Lee Evans with 379. With his total on 359 at 29.10.02, how on earth could he claim a further 20 spp. in November and December – particularly as he claimed to have seen 221 in January? There simply cannot have been enough winter birds left to see. He calls me a cheat; I call him a cheat – still the world keeps going round and still he has lost. It must hurt like hell. Ade, 5.1.03.'

In the end, it matters not a jot.

Chapter 12

Epilogue

The Enterprise ended the year about 78,000 miles older and I am now £8,000 poorer. Lee Evans is apparently continuing to add to his list for 2002 – despite the fact that the year finished several months ago.

Would I do it again? Yes, if someone paid me and bought me a car, so I guess it's unlikely. Leeds United narrowly avoided extinction at the hands of the administrators and Lee's United returned to the top of the league in 2003. I am now working on a book on butterflies – a group of animals that I have loved and studied for almost 35 years. I was told recently that Lee has placed himself at the top of the Surfbirds butterfly life-list league (in which I do not compete) and is also working on a book on butterflies. Let the games begin.

Further adventures of the Silver-haired Man

The overall critical response to *Arrivals and Rivals: a Birding Oddity* has been extremely positive. Complete strangers have thanked me for writing the book and have told me how much they enjoyed it. To each of these I extend my heart-felt thanks. As I had hoped, the subject of sport cropped up many times in conversation. England's Rugby Union team did indeed develop into a great side – eventually winning the World Cup. Our cricketers regained the ashes (though I think the tidal wave of MBE's awarded to the staff was a little over the top) and the dismantlement of my beloved Leeds United Football Club descended into a farce that culminated in near-extinction at the hands of financial administrators (twice!). I have gained a great deal of amusement from the occasional hushed whisper from behind a pair of binoculars 'Hi, Adrian (It *is* Adrian, isn't it? The bloke that wrote that book?), I see Leeds won last weekend.' Reviews in the press were usually very complimentary and I particularly thank Stuart Winter of the *Sunday Express* and Richard Millington of *Birding World* for their kind words.

I hate large crowds (before you say it, no, that is not why I watch Leeds United!) and I was horrified when I was ordered to go to the claustrophobic atmosphere of the Rutland Bird Fair to do a book-signing session. Sure, there would be people there who enjoyed the book. But what if Lee and I bumped into each other? That would be awkward, to say the least. Would a boxing match be arranged by *Rare Bird Alert*, I wondered? If so, it would certainly attract a lot of attention amongst the assembled masses. In the interests of harmony I decided to secrete myself in the sanctuary of the beer tent. I didn't see Lee; everyone was extremely friendly and I got very pleasantly drunk. It was quite a day and one that I shall never forget. It was here I discovered that I had been dubbed 'The Silver-haired Man' by Mr Evans. I am sure this was meant to be less than complimentary, but I actually quite like it and it causes great mirth amongst my friends and acquaintances. It even gave me the title for this extra chapter, which my publishers have requested for the second edition of *Arrivals*. Apparently some of you want to know what I've been up to since the 'Great Crusade'. Be careful what you wish for!

I recently heard from a friend of mine that the official Rarities Committee had accepted the female Bufflehead I saw at Great Livermere in Suffolk on 15th June 2002. This amusing (to me) turn of events meant that I could now claim an amended total of 381 species for that year. I never found out whether Lee saw the bird and, frankly, I don't really care. However, it is frustrating to think that my total was just two birds short of the then record annual list which, in my opinion, was the property of Adrian Webb. I shall probably never again be in a position to make a serious challenge to the 'title' and so I must learn to accept the silver medal and thank my lucky stars that I am still in one piece and have regained a semblance of sanity.

During the months that followed my adventure I took very little interest in twitching. One might almost say that I was 'twitched out'. I even refused several opportunities to see species that I had never seen before (Red-throated Flycatcher, *Ficedula albicilla*, and Audouin's Gull, *Larus audouinii*, come most readily to mind). This was an unfortunate side effect of the intensity of the previous year's lunacy and one that I regret suffering. On the plus side, though, the pleasure of rediscovering the joy of searching for unusual birds in my local haunts was something of a relief. I remember well saying to myself on many occasions towards the end of 2002 'I never want to see another bird in my life!' In the dark days of winter I now look forward with renewed vigour to warm spring rambles along the coastal path between Snettisham and Heacham. After the sultry summer I feel a great excitement at the prospect of finding a 'good' autumn warbler in Holkham Woods. If I do stumble across something interesting, then all well and good. But if I don't I now feel comforted by the knowledge that it matters not. I have been fortunate enough to discover many birds beneath these more relaxed skies – for example Icterine, Yellow-browed, Pallas' and Greenish Warblers, Wryneck and Ring Ouzels a-plenty. Each has given me more excitement and pleasure than any of those that I acquired from the hard work of other birders on my exploits of 2002. This is 'real' birding. One is hopefully adding to our knowledge of the timing of migrations and also helping to bring pleasure to other people by giving them the opportunity of seeing somewhat rarer species.

In general though, birds have been far less of a priority for me in recent times. I have never been able to stand still and I am always looking forward to embracing the next challenge with an ardour bordering on obsession. I didn't have long to wait. I mentioned at the end of *Arrivals* that I was starting work on a butterfly book (*British and Irish Butterflies*, 2007, Brambleby Books). A nice gentle little project after the traumas of 2002? It should have been...

Seeing all of the British butterfly species in a single calendar year was not challenge enough. There are fewer than sixty species and their whereabouts are easy enough to discover. I was birding in Holkham Woods, with my pals Jason Chapman and Phil Gould, when the latter suggested including the subspecies. To my knowledge, the only person who was familiar with the distribution and whereabouts of the British and Irish butterfly subspecies was my long-term mentor and friend Bernard Skinner (author of the book *A Colour Identification Guide to the Moths of the British Isles*, 1998, Viking, Harmondsworth,). Phil had aroused my enthusiasm but first I needed to know a little more about the challenge. I would hold on calling Bernard for advice until I had done my homework. Bernard does not suffer fools gladly and can identify one from a great distance. The first port of call was the latest authoritative list (Bradley, J., 2000, *Checklist of the Lepidoptera recorded from the British Isles*. Privately published). This suggested that, along with the scarce immigrants, there were 112 taxa to consider. Of the residents, several were found only in northern Scotland, even more only in the limestone Burren district of County Clare, western Ireland and one only in the Isle of Rhum. No-one had ever photographed them all before. Best go and buy myself a camera, then! I had never even owned one before. The acrid smell of a leather glove slapped my cheeks in invitation to a duel.

I won't bore you with the details of how the project was undertaken but I think it is relevant to explain how my experiences as a birding twitcher in 2002 helped its progress.

Firstly, I discovered that, if one wants to achieve difficult goals, there is no substitute for sheer bloody-minded determination. There is simply no room for 'I can't possibly do that.' Professional and domestic commitments aside, yes, you damned well can. If your diary says that you need to be in western Ireland tomorrow, and the weather is set fair, then get out of bed at midnight and get on the road. Get to Fishguard at 6 a.m., drive the four hours across the island and by early afternoon you'll be eye to compound eye with your quarry. If the short-term weather forecast was correct you will have a satchel full of photographs, some of which may be unique. If you book a flight several days in advance, who knows what the volatile Atlantic air currents (perhaps contrary to the long-term forecast) will dump on County Clare upon your arrival? One simply *must* be flexible, ready to go and be prepared to take *any* short-term advantage of good weather.

Secondly, prepare your year. By the end of January have a diary written, week-by-week, of where you need to be. This is a great blueprint for success as it should leave no silly little errors waiting for regrets. 'Oh! I knew I should have done that.' 'Rubbish,' as Geoffrey Boycott might say. 'Why didn't you then? That's bad technique, is that.'

Thirdly, construct a table of exactly what your targets are and why. In other words, do your homework and study the animals that you seek. Pay particular attention to any snippets of information regarding their behaviour and make sure you understand how to identify them. I find it very useful to have a file containing any and all the information I can glean from the existing literature for each taxon.

Lastly, try to build up a network of contacts throughout the British Isles. County recorders are worth their weight in gold. On many occasions, when I have been in unfamiliar territory, I have avoided failure by making a phone call to the relevant local expert. All of them have been only too pleased to help and some have even met me in the field to lend a hand.

To illustrate the importance of these points I recount below some of the more bizarre events that befell me during the four-year long butterfly project.

The 28th July 2004 found me at Carnsore Point in County Wexford, Ireland. The ferry crossing that morning had passed without gastric event, but I was very tired after the preceding seven-hour drive. A little sleep was called for but excitement at the prospect of visiting the Burren precluded this. I felt like a little boy on Christmas Eve, lying awake in eager anticipation of Santa Claus's visit. On this particular occasion, I hoped that he would bring me the two subspecies of Grayling that are endemic to the island. It was still early in the day but the prospects did not look good as the weather was overcast and cool. A single Irish Meadow Brown winced at me through the chilly breeze as I disturbed him from his slumbers. This was a good start as I had not photographed, or even seen the subspecies before. A light drizzle began as I decided to start the long drive to the Burren. I knew that it would take me at least four hours. It took nearly six. I had a car full of food and drinks, a stove on which to make coffee and a large supply of Hamlet cigars. What more could I need? Well, some Euros would have been handy! In my fatigue and excitement I had forgotten to visit the Bureau de Change whilst on the ferry.

Amidst an opaque cloud of verbal self-abuse, I parked the warm tyres of my steed on the unforgiving limestone of the

Burren and resigned myself to a night in the car. I knew from experience that, without the correct currency, taking a night's lodgings would be inviting a financial rip-off. The light drizzle became a steady drizzle. A fitful night became a horrendous morning. It was cold and the rain drifted across the leaden landscape in sheets. As the day wore on it was obvious that things were not going to improve and domestic duties meant that I could not sit this one out. I would have to drive home with more or less an empty camera. A single irritable Meadow Brown was scant reward for my efforts.

On the 4th August, just a few days after my failure in Ireland, I arrived in the Isles of Scilly. Between here and my return from the Republic I had been to northern England and southern Scotland on two separate day-visits. My presence at home was required on the nights between and so I could not stay for a single extended visit. By now the pressure of so much driving was beginning to tell. The sun and heat in the Scillies was relentless. Thankfully, the endemic subspecies of Speckled Wood and Meadow Brown were easy to find and so my marathon day-trip from Norfolk ended in success. However, it was clear to me that physically I was declining rapidly. I arrived home in time for 'Last Orders' and enjoyed a relaxing pint. So relaxing in fact that the landlord had to wake me up before ordering me home.

The following day I had to attend a Trustees meeting of the Norfolk Ornithologists' Association. On driving to the meeting I was horrified to discover that I had almost lost the vision in one eye and that one of my hands would not grip the steering wheel, no matter how hard I told it to. On my return home I tried to eat some lunch and actually dropped my fork as the muscles in my arm simply gave up the ghost. Evidently I was in serious trouble. This opinion was shared by my doctor and I found myself whisked off to Norfolk and Norwich Hospital. The diagnosis? A mini-stroke brought on by stress, too much driving, too many cigars, too much cider, too little sleep and an appalling diet of food eaten 'on the run'. I still had a trip to Martin Down in Hampshire to undertake and, fortunately, my friends drove me there. Had I driven I surely would have been a danger to everyone on the road. Would I actually have done it? I guess we shall never know. I could now look forward to the winter break as the season was at an end. I had to hope that, by the spring of 2005, I would be well enough to continue with the project. Fortunately, I was.

By the end of the 2004 season I had been given Lyme Disease by a very generous tick in the Isle of Rhum, had, through rank stupidity, got myself stranded up a mountain in the most abominable weather imaginable (twice!) and had been given a severe medical tongue-lashing about my general physical and mental well-being ('Take this as a warning, Mr Riley. You *have* to slow down.'). In retrospect, I feel that most of the strain relating to the latter had come from being ill-prepared. I had been shooting from the hip and chasing shadows. It was clear that I had to do some serious homework over the winter so that I could focus my efforts more efficiently during the following year. From the aforementioned litany of tragedies though, one thing had become quite obvious – this was not going to be an easy project.

During the winter break I created a diary, week for week that told me exactly what I needed to be looking for as the season progressed. I studied the taxonomy of each subspecies and made a file containing descriptions of each so that I could be sure of photographing individuals that conformed as closely as possible to the 'type' specimen. I also needed to know exactly *where* to look. I therefore built up a large network of contacts who very kindly gave me details of the sites I would need to visit. During my correspondence it became ever clearer that knowledge of the butterfly subspecies was scant amongst most local recorders. This fired my enthusiasm to even greater heights as I now felt that, by bringing the subject to wider public attention, I was doing something potentially very useful. I also made a checklist containing all the photographs I would need to take to show the relevant identification features. As the start of the next season approached, all of these files, along with a multitude of county lists and reference books, transformed the back of my car into a mobile office. I was ready to go. As I think Arnold Schwarzenegger once said, 'Lock and load!'

Flexibility was still going to be a vital element in the success of the mission. I was to study the weather with the ever-increasing meteorological skill that would enable me to make sound decisions regarding the timing of trips. I found long-term forecasts to be of little use and potentially disastrous. I therefore concentrated only on 24-hour predictions and made myself ready and willing to leave home at a moment's notice. This greatly increased my success rate and was evidently the only attitude to adopt if the 'day' was to be won. One very good example of an alternative tactic illustrates well the dangers of inflexibility.

Towards the end of May 2005, I received a call from my wonderful friends Alex and Gill McLennan. They wanted me to travel with them to the Burren in search of the many indigenous butterfly subspecies found there. As I had visited this geographically almost surreal site the previous year I was familiar with the region and knew exactly where to go for each butterfly. If I acted as their guide they would pay for all my expenses. This was an offer I simply could not refuse. I love this other-worldly place so much that, to the sound of David Bowie's *Space Oddity*, I would happily die there. However, I could see a large black cloud on the horizon when Alex told me that we were to fly and hire a car on arrival in Ireland. This meant booking the flight well in advance of the trip. What would the weather be like when we got there? I worried about this until the moment I saw the rain lashing down as we disembarked at Shannon airport. The time for worry was over. I slipped into something resembling panic.

We had three days in the Burren and all we could do was hope that we were blessed with at least *some* good weather. I needed only one photograph, but my friends would be heartbroken if the trip was a washout. We spent our time driving around the 'lunar' landscape praying for the thermometer to read above 13°C (the temperature threshold for doing an official butterfly transect and therefore an indication that something might be on the wing). On one occasion it did and we rushed around all of my known sites. The good weather lasted for only half a day and that was it.

Fortunately, Alex and Gill got almost all the pictures they wanted. They thoroughly enjoyed their bugging, revelled in the nightlife that was filled with the strains of Irish folk music and Alex and I were treated to a Liverpool victory in the European Champions League final – despite, at one point, 'The Reds' being 3-0 behind. On the final morning I still needed a photo of a female Irish Orange-tip. Fortunately, and despite the still inclement weather, I got one. But to get it I had to wade into a bog (also inhabited by cattle that used it as a public convenience) amidst instructions to my companions that if I failed they should catch their return flight to England and leave me to find my own way home. To this day Alex and Gill do not think I was serious. I can assure them, and you, that I was.

Even armed with a stubbornness rivalling that of a donkey with a hangover, an address and phone book the size of a small Bible and with every scrap of information I could gather, I approached August 2005, still needing photos of the aforementioned Grayling subspecies from Ireland. On every previous journey I found myself sitting in the car listening to the rain hammering on the roof of the car. If I didn't get these on this fifth visit to the Republic, I would have to extend the fieldwork into a fourth year and, more importantly, would have to wait a *whole* year to find this late-emerging species and atone for my previous failures. This would be disastrous. I had secured a publishing deal and needed the book to come out on time. After all, there is the much-needed income from royalties to think about!

I made my way to the Burren and sat in the rain for a day and a night. My diary reads *'I've been here before!!!'* By now I had not had any decent sleep for the equivalent of three days and was beginning to recognize the signs of exhaustion: shaking hands, abstract thought processes and talking out loud to myself being three sure symptoms. Add to this the fear of yet another failure and we had a pretty poorly Adrian on our hands. The following dawn was greeted by a watery sun from the east and my spirits soared with the prospect of success sailing across the pastel sky. I took my first walk atop the treacherous limestone pavement at 7.30 a.m. The air was chilly and, on returning to the car about half an hour later, I realized that I needed to calm my eagerness. A cup of coffee and a smoke was in order. My next walk was punctuated by butterfly after butterfly and most of them were the fabled Burren Grayling. The relief and joy that I felt was painful. A knot the size of a fist gripped my stomach and reminded me that not only was I suffering from sleep depravation but also lack of food. Loss of appetite is another symptom of exhaustion; I had hardly eaten since arriving in Ireland. Flushed with early victory (I was now two hours ahead of my schedule for the day) I went back to the car, ate a large breakfast and 'power slept' for an hour. I woke feeling like a king and was ready to make the long journey to the Dingle peninsular for the last crusade. I now needed just a single photograph to complete an arduous and, to my knowledge, unique achievement.

I arrived at the peninsular amidst glorious sunshine and my hopes were as high as the scant, negligee-like wisps of summer cloud. Bernard had given me directions, extracted from his diaries from the 1970's, for the colony of graylings. Would they still be there 30 years later? I was to look for a small piece of moorland just north of Dunquin. There was no shortage of moorland, though most I would have described as heathland, similar to that in parts of the New Forest, Hampshire. Still, the New Forest is great for graylings so I should be okay. After about three hours of unsuccessful searching, it was clear that I had somehow made a huge mistake. My mobile phone was not working and I could not call Bernard as I had done many times before when in Scotland to clarify the whereabouts of the site and I had very little time left before I simply *had* to set off on the return journey. Was I to be beaten for the want of a single photo after so much effort? I was utterly downhearted and dejected. Tears of frustration welled in my eyes and my throat felt as if I had swallowed a snooker ball. But there was nothing for it: I had to leave my prize behind.

Reluctantly, I pulled my car off the car park and headed disconsolately towards Dunquin. Shortly after doing so, I noticed to my right an area that I supposed could have been described as moorland and, as Bernard had detailed, it was adjacent to the sea. As I drove slowly past it I decided that it did not look like a 'typical' grayling site. Hundred yards, two hundred yards – the car rolled on. Suddenly it dawned on me that I was not looking for a 'typical' grayling. Alarm bells rang in my head. This subspecies has a much darker underside than its English counterpart – presumably to make its camouflage more effective against a dark substrate. The sparse vegetation of the area I had just passed was growing on dark soil. In a state of near-hysteria I turned the car around and parked at the top of the moor. I scanned quickly with my binoculars and could see clearly several butterflies on the wing. When gliding they held their wings in a characteristic 'V', similar to that of a Common Buzzard. They were graylings – the Irish Graylings. From the jaws of defeat I had grasped victory. The tears that flooded then were not of frustration but of sheer ecstasy.

On the journey back to Fishguard, with my phone now back in action, I sent the following text to all my friends and colleagues: 'I am now the first person to have photographed all the species and subspecies of butterfly found in Great Britain and Ireland.' As I type these words, and recall the moment, I can again feel my throat tighten with the emotion experienced that day. I have known nothing like it before or since.

As many of my projects do, this one evolved and grew into something akin to Frankenstein's monster. The initial idea was simply to *see* all the subspecies in a single year. With the limited knowledge I had of their geographical distributions, it soon became clear that my goal would take two years. At this point, I also realized that no-one had ever before *photographed* all of these butterflies. By the end of the second season, I was 'looking forward' to the third and, by the start of the fourth, I could finally see the end in sight. If this isn't sheer, bloody-minded determination then I don't know what is. Perhaps some would call it obsession, and I can well understand that viewpoint. But however one describes it, I think it is a necessary prerequisite if one is to take on the best-known, and probably most successful, bird twitcher in the UK or undertake the field research for a book. Unfortunately, this latest project, and my unceasing commitment to it, went a long way to costing me my marriage. So beware: although in these pages I have encouraged total commitment, one must always remember that one's partner may not share that same enthusiasm and the cost of ignoring the fact may be extremely high!

I am now working on an identification guide to the British and Irish dragonflies and damselflies. At the start of 2007, having done my preparatory work, I needed 167 photographs. As the summer draws to a close and my attention begins to turn once again to autumn birding, I need 52. Not a bad start. Let's see what 2008 has in store. Visit www.enterprise-io.co.uk to view the Photogallery, compiled by *'Team io'*, showing many more birds and butterflies than are presented in this book.

The List

So here it is – the bit most readers will have been waiting for. I wonder how many have skipped straight to this section and ignored the rest of the book? Some of the records are in the hands of the BBRC and some may subsequently be rejected. Even so, I have included them here for the reasons outlined in Chapter 11. In this second edition, the Bufflehead has been added to the list (see Chapter 13). The systematic order and specific nomenclature follow that of Beaman, M. & Madge, S. (1998). *The Handbook of Bird Identification for Europe and the Western Palearctic.* Helm, London.

Butterflies mentioned in the book are listed at the end of this chapter, including their Latin names.

1. **Red-throated Diver**, *Gavia stellata*; several throughout the British Isles
2. **Black-throated Diver**, *Gavia arctica*; several in Scotland
3. **Great Northern Diver**, *Gavia immer*; several throughout the British Isles
4. **White-billed Diver**, *Gavia adamsii*; Durness, Sutherland, 30th May (one)
5. **Little Grebe**, *Tachybaptus ruficollis*; frequent
6. **Great Crested Grebe**, *Podiceps cristatus*; frequent
7. **Red-necked Grebe**, *Podiceps grisegena*; Largo Bay, Fifeshire, 10th Feb. (one); Fen Drayton, Cambs., 18th May (one)
8. **Slavonian Grebe**, *Podiceps auritus*; Holme, Norfolk, 14th Feb. (one); Titchwell, Norfolk, 5th Nov. (one)
9. **Black-necked Grebe**, *Podiceps nigricollis*; Largo Bay, Fifeshire, 10th Feb. (one); Studland, Dorset, 21st Feb. (three); Lackford, Norfolk, 27th March (two)

10. Fulmar, *Fulmarus glacialis*; frequent
11. Cory's Shearwater, *Calonectris diomedea*; St. Mary's / Penzance, Cornwall, 15th June (two)
12. Great Shearwater, *Puffinus gravis*; off St Mary's, Cornwall, 14th Aug. (seven)
13. Sooty Shearwater, *Puffinus griseus*; several, Cornwall, Norfolk, Hebrides
14. Manx Shearwater, *Puffinus puffinus*; common, Cornwall, Norfolk, Hebrides
15. Balearic Shearwater, *Puffinus yelkouan*; Portland, Dorset, 11th March (one); Penzance, Cornwall, 13th Aug. (two); Cley, Norfolk, 27th Aug. (two)
16. Wilson's Storm-petrel, *Oceanites oceanus*; Penzance / St Mary's, Cornwall, 13th Aug. (one); off St Mary's, Cornwall, 14th Aug. (seven +)
17. European Storm-petrel, *Hydrobates pelagicus*; off St Mary's, Cornwall, 14th Aug. (20+)
18. Leach's Storm-petrel, *Oceanodroma leucorhoa*; Cley, Norfolk, 27th Aug. (three)
19. Gannet, *Morus bassanus*; frequent
20. Cormorant, *Phalacrocorax carbo*; common
21. Shag, *Phalacrocorax aristotelis*; common, Scotland; Cornwall
22. Bittern, *Botaurus stellaris*; Abberton Res., Essex, 11th Jan. (one); Lea Valley, Herts., 11th Jan. (one); Cley, Norfolk, 28th July (one)
23. Night Heron, *Nycticorax nycticorax*; Tregeseal, Cornwall, 26th March (one)
24. Squacco Heron, *Ardeola ralloides*; Barrow-in-Furness, Cumbria, 8th June (one)
25. Cattle Egret, *Bulbulcus ibis*; Gweek, Cornwall, 25th & 26th

March (three)
26. **Little Egret**, *Egretta garzetta*; frequent. Norfolk, Suffolk, Cornwall, Kent
27. **Snowy Egret**, *Egretta thula*; Castleton Bay, Argyll, 31st May (one)
28. **Great White Egret**, *Egretta alba*; Hemsby, Norfolk, 19th Feb. (one)
29. **Grey Heron**, *Ardea cinerea*; common throughout
30. **Purple Heron**, *Ardea purpurea*; Holme, Norfolk, 22nd May (one)
31. **Black Stork**, *Ciconia nigra*; near Stibbard, Norfolk, 26th May (one)
32. **White Stork**, *Ciconia ciconia*; Findern, Derbyshire, 10th Feb. (one); Acle, Norfolk, 26th April (one)
33. **Glossy Ibis**, *Plegadis falcinellus*; Budleigh Salterton, Devon, 7th Sept. (one)
34. **Spoonbill**, *Platalea leucorodia*; several; Norfolk, Cleveland, Devon
35. **Mute Swan**, *Cygnus olor*; common
36. **Bewick's Swan**, *Cygnus columbianus*; Abberton Res., Essex, 11th Jan. (five); many Norfolk/Cambs.
37. **Whooper Swan**, *Cygnus cygnus*; several; Essex, Norfolk/Cambs., Ayrshire, Wexford
38. **Tundra Bean Goose**, *Anser rossicus*; Abberton Res., Essex, 11th Jan. (22); Stiffkey, Norfolk, 21st Jan. (six) & 29th Dec. (two)
39. **Taiga Bean Goose**, *Anser fabalis*; several; Cantley Marshes, Norfolk, Jan. & Nov.
40. **Pink-footed Goose**, *Anser brachyrhynchus*; thousands in Norfolk; also Aberdeenshire, Dumfries, Wexford
41. **European White-fronted Goose**, *Anser albifrons*; frequent

in Norfolk
42. **Greenland White-fronted Goose**, *Anser flavirostris*; Loch Ken, Dumfries, 8th Feb. (41)
43. **Greylag Goose**, *Anser anser*; common throughout England and Scotland
44. **Snow Goose**, *Anser caerulescens*; Loch of Strathbeg, Aberdeenshire, 9th Feb. (one); Holkham, Norfolk, 17th Oct. (one)
45. **Ross's Goose**, *Anser rossii*; Holkham, Norfolk, 28th Jan. (one)
46. **Canada Goose**, *Branta canadensis*; common throughout
47. **Barnacle Goose**, *Branta leucopsis*; Caerlaverock, Dumfries, 8th Feb. (*c.*1000); several feral birds, Norfolk
48. **Dark-bellied Brent Goose**, *Branta bernicla*; common; Norfolk, Suffolk, Essex
49. **Pale-bellied Brent Goose**, *Branta hrota*; Cockthorpe, Norfolk, 24th Jan. (two)
50. **Black Brant**, *Branta nigricans*; Holkham, Norfolk, 21st Jan. (one); Titchwell, Norfolk, 1st March & 7th May (one)
51. **Red-breasted Goose**, *Branta ruficollis*; Holkham, Norfolk, 21st Jan. (one)
52. **Egyptian Goose**, *Alopochen aegyptiacus*; frequent in Norfolk
53. **Ruddy Shelduck**, *Tadorna ferruginea*; several, Norfolk
54. **Shelduck**, *Tadorna tadorna*; common
55. **Mandarin Duck**, *Aix galericulata*; Holkham, Norfolk, 21st Jan. (one); Heacham, Norfolk, 17th April (a pair); several Berkshire
56. **Eurasian Wigeon**, *Anas penelope*; common
57. **American Wigeon**, *Anas americana*; Loch Martnaham, Ayrshire, 8th Feb. (one)

58. **Falcated Duck**, *Anas falcata*; Minsmere, Suffolk, 10th June (one)
59. **Gadwall**, *Anas strepera*; frequent
60. **Common Teal**, *Anas crecca*; common
61. **Green-winged Teal**, *Anas carolinensis*; Warwickdale Marsh, Ayrshire, 8th Feb. (one)
62. **Mallard**, *Anas platyrhynchos*; common
63. **Black Duck**, *Anas rubripes*; Slapton Ley, Devon, 11th March (one)
64. **Pintail**, *Anas acuta*; frequent
65. **Garganey**, *Anas querquedula*; several, Norfolk
66. **Blue-winged Teal**, *Anas discors*; Cotswold Water Park, Wilts., 1st Oct. (one)
67. **Baikal Teal**, *Anas formosa*; Stanton Harcourt, Oxon., 24th Dec. (one)
68. **Shoveler**, *Anas clypeata;* frequent
   [**Marbled Duck**, *Marmaronetta angustirostris;* Netherton, Yorkshire, 2nd Aug. (one presumed escapee)]
69. **Red-crested Pochard**, *Netta rufina*; Stockers Lake, Herts., 9th Jan. (two); Cotswold Water Park, Wilts., 15th April (one)
70. **Pochard**, *Aythya ferina*; common
71. **Canvasback**, *Aythya valisineria*; Pennington Flash, Lancashire, 23rd July (one)
72. **Redhead**, *Aythya americana*; Kenfig, Glamorgan, 3rd Jan. (one)
73. **Ring-necked Duck**, *Aythya collaris*; Low Barnes, Durham, 10th Feb. (one)
74. **Ferruginous Duck**, *Aythya nyroca*; Elstow, Beds., 9th Jan. (one)
75. **Tufted Duck**, *Aythya fuligula*; common
76. **Scaup**, *Aythya marila*; several; Fifeshire, Dorset

77. **Lesser Scaup**, *Aythya affinis*; Littlesea, Dorset, 21st Feb. (one)
78. **Eider**, *Somateria mollissima*; frequent
79. **King Eider**, *Somateria spectabilis*; Holkham and Wells, Norfolk, 23rd Feb. (one)
80. **Long-tailed Duck**, *Clangula hyemalis*; several; Norfolk, Fifeshire and Orkney
81. **Common Scoter**, *Melanitta nigra*; frequent
82. **Black Scoter**, *Melanitta americana*; Llanfairfechan, Conwy, 2nd April (one)
83. **Surf Scoter**, *Melanitta perspicillata*; Largo Bay, Fifeshire, 10th Feb. (two); Titchwell, Norfolk, 18th June (one)
84. **Velvet Scoter**, *Melanitta fusca*; several; Norfolk and Fifeshire
85. **Bufflehead**, *Bucephala albeola*; Great Livermere, Suffolk, 15th June (one)
86. **Goldeneye**, *Bucephala clangula*; frequent
87. **Smew**, *Mergellus albellus*; Stocker's Lake, Herts., 9th Jan. (three); Loch Martnaham, Ayrshire, 8th Feb. (a pair)
88. **Red-breasted Merganser**, *Mergus serrator*; Frequent
89. **Goosander**, *Mergus merganser*; several; Herts., Ayrshire, Dumfries.
90. **Ruddy Duck**, *Oxyura jamaicensis*; several; Norfolk and Cleveland
91. **White-headed Duck**, *Oxyura leucocephala*; Harley Flood, Norfolk, 21st June (one)
92. **Honey Buzzard**, *Pernis apivorus*; frequent at Great Ryburgh, Norfolk
93. **Black Kite**, *Milvus migrans*; Heacham, Norfolk, 5th April (one)
94. **Red Kite**, *Milvus milvus*; Dollgellau, Gwynedd, 16th Feb.

(one)
95. **White-tailed Eagle**, *Haliaetus albicilla*; Gruinard Bay, Rosshire (one)
96. **Marsh Harrier**, *Circus aeruginosus*; frequent in Norfolk and Suffolk
97. **Hen Harrier**, *Circus cyaneus*; frequent in Norfolk
98. **Pallid Harrier**, *Circus macrourus*; Elmley, Kent, 11th Aug. (one); Warham, Norfolk, from 28th Dec.
99. **Montagu's Harrier**, *Circus pygargus*; three in north Norfolk during May
100. **Goshawk**, *Accipiter gentiles*; three in Thetford Forest, Suffolk, 4th Feb.; 30th Mar.; 7th May
101. **Sparrowhawk**, *Accipiter nisus*; frequent
102. **Common Buzzard**, *Buteo buteo*; common
103. **Rough-legged Buzzard**, *Buteo lagopus*; Haddiscoe, Norfolk, Jan. & Feb. (one)
104. **Golden Eagle**, *Aquila chrysaetos*; Glenshee, Aberdeens., 10th Feb. (one); Loch Druidibeg, S. Uist, 28th May (one)
105. **Osprey**, *Pandion haliaetus*; several; Invernesshire. Also Rutland Water, Rutland, 16th April; Acle, Norfolk, 26th April (one).
106. **Lesser Kestrel**, *Falco naumannii*; Peninnis, St Mary's, I.o.Scilly, 20th May (one)
107. **Kestrel**, *Falco tinnunculus*; frequent throughout
108. **Red-footed Falcon**, *Falco vespertinus*; Salthouse Heath, Norfolk, 19th May (one)
109. **Merlin**, *Falco columbarius*; several; Norfolk, Rosshire, Sutherland
110. **Hobby**, *Falco subbuteo*; several; Norfolk, Staffs., Kent
111. **Peregrine**, *Falco peregrinus*; frequent
112. **Red Grouse**, *Lagopus lagopus* ssp. *scoticus*; Glenshee,

Aberdeenshire, 10th Feb. (common)

113. **Ptarmigan**, *Lagopus mutus*; Glenshee, Aberdeenshire, 10th Feb. (five)
114. **Black Grouse**, *Tetrao tetrix*; Abernethy Forest, Inverness, 9th Feb. (two)
115. **Capercaillie**, *Tetrao urogallus*; Abernethy Forest, Inverness, 9th Feb. (one)
116. **Red-legged Partridge**, *Alectoris rufa*; common in Norfolk
117. **Grey Partridge**, *Perdix perdix*; frequent in Norfolk; Loch of Strathbeg, Aberdeenshire, 9th Feb. (one)
118. **Quail**, *Coturnix coturnix*; several in Norfolk
119. **Common Pheasant**, *Phasianus colchicus*; common
120. **Golden Pheasant**, *Chrysolophus pictus*; several in Wayland Woods and Woolferton, Norfolk
121. **Lady Amherst's Pheasant**, *Chrysolophus amherstiae*; Little Brickhill, Beds., 21st Feb. (one)
122. **Water Rail**, *Rallus aquaticus*; frequent
123. **Spotted Crake**, *Porzana porzana*; Belvide Res., Staffs., 2nd April (one); Marazion Marsh, Cornwall, 5th Oct. (one)
124. **Corncrake**, *Crex crex*; several in Outer Hebrides
125. **Moorhen**, *Gallinula chloropus*; common
126. **Coot**, *Fulica atra*; common
127. **Common Crane**, *Grus grus*; several in Norfolk
128. **Oystercatcher**, *Haematopus ostralegus*; common
129. **Black-winged Stilt**, *Himantopus himantopus*; one at Titchwell, Norfolk, throughout the year
130. **Avocet**, *Recurvirostra avosetta*; frequent in Norfolk
131. **Stone Curlew**, *Burhinus oedicnemus*; several in Thetford Forest, Suffolk
132. **Little Ringed Plover**, *Charadrius dubius*; several; Norfolk, Suffolk, Yorkshire

133. Ringed Plover, *Charadrius hiaticula*; common throughout
134. Killdeer, *Charadrius vociferus*; St Agnes, I.o.Scilly, Cornwall, 7th Nov. (one)
135. Kentish Plover, *Charadrius alexandrinus*; Oare Marshes, Kent, 29th April (one)
136. Lesser Sand Plover, *Charadrius mongolus*; Rimac, Lincs., 12th May (one)
137. Dotterell, *Charadrius morinellus*; North Cave, Yorkshire, 16th April (three)
138. American Golden Plover, *Pluvialis dominica*; Home Fen, Cambs., 8th Nov. (one)
139. Pacific Golden Plover, *Pluvialis fulva*; Horseshoe Point, Lincs., 18th July (one)
140. European Golden Plover, *Pluvialis apricaria*; common
141. Grey Plover, *Pluvialis squatarola*; common
142. Lapwing, *Vanellus vanellus*; common
143. Knot, *Calidris canutus*; common in Norfolk
144. Sanderling, *Calidris alba*; frequent in Norfolk
145. Little Stint, *Calidris minuta*; several; Norfolk, Wilts., Kent, Cheshire
146. Temminck's Stint, *Calidris temminckii*; Mickle Mere, Suffolk, 8th May (one); Cley, Norfolk, 14th May (one)
147. Least Sandpiper, *Calidris minutilla*; Drayton Basset, Staffs., 24th May (one)
148. White-rumped Sandpiper, *Calidris fuscicollis*; Cresswell Ponds, Northumberland, 30th June (one); Titchwell, Norfolk, 24th July & 1st Sep. (one)
149. Pectoral Sandpiper, *Calidris melanotos*; Pensthorpe, Norfolk, 24th July (one); Foula, Shetlands, 25th Sep. (one)
150. Curlew Sandpiper, *Calidris ferruginea*; several at Cley and Titchwell, Norfolk

151. Purple Sandpiper, *Calidris maritime*; Titchwell, Norfolk, 28th Jan. (one); Salthouse, Norfolk, 13th Nov. (two)
152. Dunlin, *Calidris alpina*; common
153. Broad-billed Sandpiper, *Limicola falcinellus*; Cley, Norfolk, 3rd Aug. (two)
154. Stilt Sandpiper, *Micropalama himantopus*; Pennington Marshes, Hants., 22nd July (one)
155. Buff-breasted Sandpiper, *Tryngites subruficollis*; Wheldrake Ings, Yorks., 26th Sep. (one)
156. Ruff, *Philomachus pugnax*; frequent in Norfolk
157. Jack Snipe, *Lymnocryptes minimus*; several; Norfolk, I.o.Scilly, Shetland
158. Snipe, *Gallinago gallinago*; frequent
159. Great Snipe, *Gallinago media*; Blakeney Point, Norfolk, 12th Sep. (one)
160. Long-billed Dowitcher, *Limnodromus scolopaceus*; Foula, Shetland, 25th Sep. (one)
161. Woodcock, *Scolopax rusticola*; several; Beds., Aberdeenshire, Norfolk
162. Black-tailed Godwit, *Limosa limosa*; frequent in Norfolk
163. Bar-tailed Godwit, *Limosa lapponica*; frequent in Norfolk
164. Whimbrel, *Numenius phaeopus*; frequent
165. Curlew, *Numenius arquata*; common
166. Spotted Redshank, *Tringa erythropus*; frequent in Norfolk
167. Redshank, *Tringa tetanus*; Common
168. Marsh Sandpiper, *Tringa stagnatilis*; Leventhorpe Flash, Yorks., 8th June (one)
169. Greenshank, *Tringa nebularia*; frequent
170. Lesser Yellowlegs, *Tringa flavipes*; Frodsham Marsh, Cheshire, 21st March (one); Cantley, Norfolk, 13th Nov. (one)

171. Solitary Sandpiper, *Tringa solitaria*; Rye Meads, Herts., 14th Sep. (one)
172. Green Sandpiper, *Tringa ochropus*; frequent in Norfolk
173. Wood Sandpiper, *Tringa glareola*; several; Heacham, Stiffkey and Cley, Norfolk
174. Terek Sandpiper, *Xenus cinereus*; Malden, Essex, 25th Aug. (one)
175. Common Sandpiper, *Actitis hypoleucos*; frequent
176. Spotted Sandpiper, *Actitis macularia*; Derwent Water, Durham, 20th June (one)
177. Turnstone, *Arenaria interpres*; frequent
178. Red-necked Phalarope, *Phalaropus lobatus*; Stiffkey, Norfolk, 23rd May (one); Loch Fada, North Uist, 28th May (three)
179. Grey Phalarope, *Phalaropus fulicaria*; Titchwell, Norfolk, 26th Sep. (one); Penzance / St Mary's, Cornwall, 5th Oct. (three)
180. Pomarine Skua, *Stercorarius pomarinus*; Kessingland, Suffolk, 27th Feb. (one); Marazion, Cornwall, 20th May (three); Uig / Lochmaddy, Skye, 27th May (35) & 29th May (three); Shetland Mainland, 20th Sep. (one)
181. Arctic Skua, *Stercorarius parasiticus*; frequent; Norfolk and Scotland
182. Long-tailed Skua, *Stercorarius longicaudus*; Uig / Lochmaddy, 27th May (two); Cley, Norfolk, 6th Aug. (two)
183. Great Skua, *Catharacta skua*; frequent; Norfolk, Cornwall, Scotland
184. Mediterranean Gull, *Larus melanocephalus*; several; Norfolk, Devon, Lancs., I. o. Scilly
185. Franklin's Gull, *Larus pipixcan*; Farmoor, Oxon., 18th Aug. (one)

186. Little Gull, *Larus minutes*; several; Norfolk, Kent, Cleveland
187. Sabine's Gull, *Larus sabini*; Ceann a' Gharaidh, South Uist, 28th May (one)
188. Bonaparte's Gull, *Larus philadelphia*; Millbrook, Devon, 2nd Feb. (one)
189. Black-headed Gull, *Larus ridibundus*; common
190. Ring-billed Gull, *Larus delawarensis*; Woodbridge, Suffolk, 11th Jan. (one); Stromness, Orkney, 6th Dec., (one)
191. Common Gull, *Larus canus*; frequent
192. Herring Gull, *Larus argentatus*; common
193. American Herring Gull, *Larus smithsonianus*; Corfe Mullen, Dorset, 11th March (one)
194. Lesser Black-backed Gull, *Larus fuscus*; frequent
195. Yellow-legged Gull, *Larus michahellis*; three in Norfolk; one at Stanton Harcourt, Oxon., 24th Dec.
196. Caspian Gull, *Larus cachinnans*; King's Lynn, Norfolk, 14th Feb. (one)
197. Iceland Gull, *Larus glaucoides*; Lancaster, Lancs., 16th Feb. (one); Stromness, Orkney, 6th Dec. (one)
198. Glaucous Gull, *Larus hyperboreus*; King's Lynn, Norfolk, 14th Feb. (one)
199. Great Black-backed Gull, *Larus marinus*; frequent
200. Ross's Gull, *Rhodostethia rosea*; Plym Estuary, Devon, 2nd Feb. (one)
201. Kittiwake, *Rissa tridactyla*; frequent
202. Ivory Gull, *Pagophila eburnea*; Black Rock Sands, Gwynedd, 16th Feb. (one)
203. Gull-billed Tern, *Sterna nilotica*; Drift Res., Cornwall, 3rd Sep. (one)
204. Caspian Tern, *Sterna caspia*; Hickling Broad, Norfolk, 13th

May (one)
205. Sandwich Tern, *Sterna sandvicensis*; frequent
206. Elegant Tern, *Sterna elegans*; Dingle Bay, Co. Kerry, Ireland, 26th Oct. (one)
207. Roseate Tern, *Sterna dougallii*; Dungeness, Kent, 23rd April (one); Breyden Water, Norfolk, 19th July (one)
208. Common Tern, *Sterna hirundo*; frequent
209. Arctic Tern, *Sterna paradisaea*; frequent, esp. Scotland
210. Forster's Tern, *Sterna forsteri*; Hayle Estuary, Cornwall, 27th Nov. (one)
211. Little Tern, *Sterna albifrons*; frequent
212. Whiskered Tern, *Chlidonias hybridus*; Cotswold Water Park, Wilts., 15th April (one)
213. Black Tern, *Chlidonias niger*; four in Norfolk. Lakenheath Fen, Snettisham, Cley
214. White-winged Black Tern, *Chlidonias leucopterus*; Bolton-on-Swaile, Yorks., 10th May (one); Cantley, Norfolk, 13th Nov. (one)
215. Guillemot, *Uria aalge*; frequent; common in Scotland
216. Razorbill, *Alca torda*; common in Scotland
217. Black Guillemot, *Cepphus grylle*; frequent in Scotland; Llanfairfechan, Conwy, 2nd April (one)
218. Little Auk, *Alle alle*; Cley, Norfolk, 9th Nov. (one)
219. Puffin, *Fratercula arctica*; several in Hebrides
220. Rock Dove, *Columba livia*; frequent in Outer Hebrides
221. Stock Dove, *Columba oenas*; frequent
222. Woodpigeon, *Columba palumbus*; common
223. Collared Dove, *Streptopelia decaocto*; common
224. Turtle Dove, *Streptopelia turtur*; frequent in Norfolk
225. Rufous Turtle Dove, *Streptopelia orientalis*; Stromness, Orkney, 6th Dec. (one)

226. **Ring-necked Parakeet**, *Psittacula krameri*; Wraysbury, Greater London, 9th Jan. (several); Old Hunstanton, Norfolk, 1st Sep. (one)
227. **Cuckoo**, *Cuculus canorus*; frequent
228. **Barn Owl**, *Tyto alba*; frequent, esp. Norfolk
229. **Scops Owl**, *Otus scops*; Porthgwarra, Cornwall, 25th & 26th March (one)
230. **Little Owl**, *Athene noctua*; frequent in Norfolk
231. **Tawny Owl**, *Strix aluco*; frequent
232. **Long-eared Owl**, *Asio otus*; Lea Valley, Herts., 11th Jan. (one); Walsey Hill, Norfolk, 11th April (one)
233. **Short-eared Owl**, *Asio flammeus*; several; Norfolk, Suffolk, North Uist, I.o.Scilly
234. **Nightjar**, *Caprimulgus europaeus*; several at Salthouse Heath, Norfolk, 19th June
235. **Common Swift**, *Apus apus*; common
236. **Alpine Swift**, *Apus melba*; St Just, Cornwall, 26th March (two)
237. **Kingfisher**, *Alcedo atthis*; frequent
238. **European Bee-eater**, *Merops apiaster*; Bishop Middleham, Co. Durham, 3rd June (a pair); near Langham, Norfolk, 23rd Aug. (one)
239. **Hoopoe**, *Upupa epops*; Porthgwarra, Cornwall, 25th March (one)
240. **Wryneck**, *Jynx torquilla*; Great Yarmouth, Norfolk, 28th April (one); Holkham, Norfolk, 10th Sep. (one)
241. **Green Woodpecker**, *Picus viridis*; frequent
242. **Great Spotted Woodpecker**, *Dendrocopos major*; frequent
243. **Lesser Spotted Woodpecker**, *Dendrocopos minor*; regular at Holkham Hall, Norfolk
244. **Short-toed Lark**, *Calandrella brachydactyla*; Tresco,

I.o.Scilly, 10th Oct. (one)
245. Woodlark, *Lullula arborea*; several; Norfolk, Suffolk, Devon
246. Skylark, *Alauda arvensis*; common
247. Shorelark, *Eremophila alpestris*; frequent in north Norfolk
248. Sand Martin, *Riparia riparia*; frequent
249. Swallow, *Hirundo rustica*; common
250. Red-rumped Swallow, *Hirundo daurica*; Hull, Yorks., 9th April (one)
251. House Martin, *Delichon urbica*; common
252. Richard's Pipit, *Anthus richardi*; St Mary's, I.o.Scilly, 6th Oct. (one)
253. Blyth's Pipit, *Anthus godlewskii*; Gringley Carr, Notts., 30th Dec. (one)
254. Tawny Pipit, *Anthus campestris*; Dungeness, Kent, 8th Sep. (one)
255. Olive-backed Pipit, *Anthus hodgsoni*; Lynford, Norfolk, 3rd Feb. (one)
256. Tree Pipit, *Anthus trivialis*; frequent
257. Meadow Pipit, *Anthus pratensis*; common
258. Red-throated Pipit, *Anthus cervinus*; Holkham, Norfolk, 10th Sep. (one)
259. Rock Pipit, *Anthus petrosus*; frequent
260. Water Pipit, *Anthus spinoletta*; regular at Cley, Norfolk
261. Yellow Wagtail, *Motacilla flava*; frequent
262. Citrine Wagtail, *Motacilla citreola*; Marazion, Cornwall, 20th May (one); St Martin's, I. o. Scilly, 8th Oct. (one)
263. Grey Wagtail, *Motacilla cinerea*; frequent
264. Pied Wagtail, *Motacilla yarrellii*; common
265. White Wagtail, *Motacilla alba*; several; Norfolk, I.o.Scilly
266. Waxwing, *Bombycilla garrulus*; Aviemore, Invernesshire, 9th

Feb. (five)
267. **Dipper**, *Cinclus cinclus;* Craigellachie, Moray, 9th Feb. (one)
268. **Wren**, *Troglodytes troglodytes;* common
269. **Dunnock**, *Prunella modularis;* common
270. **Alpine Accentor**, *Prunella collaris;* Minsmere, Suffolk, 17th April (one)
271. **Robin**, *Erithacus rubecula;* common
272. **Thrush Nightingale**, *Luscinia luscinia;* Spurn Head, Yorks., 10th May (one)
273. **Nightingale**, *Luscinia megarhynchos;* frequent at Salthouse Heath, Norfolk
274. **Bluethroat**, *Luscinia svecica;* Thornham Point, Norfolk, 13th May (one); St Mary's, I. o. Scilly, 12th Oct. (one)
275. **Red-flanked Bluetail**, *Tarsiger cyanurus;* Gibraltar Point, Lincs., 16th Nov. (one)
276. **Black Redstart**, *Phoenicurus ochruros;* several; Cornwall, I. o. Scilly
277. **Common Redstart**, *Phoenicurus phoenicurus;* frequent
278. **Winchat**, *Saxicola rubetra;* frequent
279. **Stonechat**, *Saxicola torquata;* frequent
280. **Wheatear**, *Oenanthe oenanthe;* frequent
281. **Black-eared Wheatear**, *Oenanthe hispanica;* Nanquidno, Cornwall, 25th March (one)
282. **Grey-cheeked Thrush**, *Catharus minimus;* Gugh, I.o.Scilly, 30th Oct. (one)
283. **Ring Ouzel**, *Turdus torquatus;* frequent; Norfolk, I.o.Scilly
284. **Blackbird**, *Turdus merula;* common
285. **Fieldfare**, *Turdus pilaris;* frequent
286. **Song Thrush**, *Turdus philomelos;* frequent
287. **Redwing**, *Turdus iliacus;* frequent

288. Mistle Thrush, *Turdus viscivorus*; frequent
289. Cetti's Warbler, *Cettia cetti*; several; Norfolk, Cornwall, Wiltshire
290. Pallas's Grasshopper Warbler, *Locustella certhiola*; Tresco, I. o. Scilly, 6th Oct. (one)
291. Grasshopper Warbler, *Locustella naevia*; several; Norfolk, Staffs.
292. River Warbler, *Locustella fluviatilis*; Fair Isle, Shetland, 23rd Sep. (one)
293. Savi's Warbler, *Locustella luscinioides*; Dungeness, Kent, 19th June (one)
294. Aquatic Warbler, *Acrocephalus paludicola*; Marazion, Cornwall, 13th Aug. (one)
295. Sedge Warbler, *Acrocephalus schoenobaenus*; frequent
296. Blyth's Reed Warbler, *Acrocephalus dumetorum*; St Mary's, I. o. Scilly, 30th Oct. (one)
297. Marsh Warbler, *Acrocephalus palustris*; Weybourne, Norfolk, 3rd June (one)
298. Reed Warbler, *Acrocephalus scirpaceus*; frequent
299. Great Reed Warbler, *Acrocephalus arundinaceus*; Frensham Little Pond, Surrey, 21st May (one)
300. Booted Warbler, *Hippolais caligata*; Portland, Dorset, 16th Aug. (one)
301. Icterine Warbler, *Hippolais icterina*; Titchwell, Norfolk, 6th June (one); Wells, Norfolk, 11th-17th Sep. (one)
302. Melodious Warbler, *Hippolais polyglotta*; Portland, Dorset, 16th Aug. (two)
303. Dartford Warbler, *Sylvia undata*; several; Suffolk, Surrey, Dorset
304. Western Subalpine Warbler, *Sylvia cantillans*; Winterton, Norfolk, 24th April (one)

305. **Sardinian Warbler**, *Sylvia melanocephala*; Old Hunstanton, Norfolk, 27th Sep. (one)
306. **Barred Warbler**, *Sylvia nisoria*; Sheringham, Norfolk, 26th Aug.-1st Sep. (one); Fair Isle, Shetland, 23rd Sep. (one)
307. **Lesser Whitethroat**, *Sylvia curruca*; frequent
308. **Common Whitethroat**, *Sylvia communis*; common
309. **Garden Warbler**, *Sylvia borin*; frequent
310. **Blackcap**, *Sylvia atricapilla*; frequent
311. **Greenish Warbler**, *Phylloscopus trochiloides*; Donna Nook, Lincs., 11th Sep. (one)
312. **Arctic Warbler**, *Phylloscopus borealis*; North Collafirth, Shetland, 24th Sep. (one)
313. **Pallas's Warbler**, *Phylloscopus proregulus*; St Mary's, I. o. Scilly, 3rd Dec. (one)
314. **Yellow-browed Warbler**, *Phylloscopus inornatus*; St Mary's, I. o. Scilly, 5th Oct. & 3rd Dec. (one); Tresco, I. o. Scilly, 6th Oct. (one); Stiffkey, Norfolk, 28-31st Dec. (one)
315. **Hume's Yellow-browed Warbler**, *Phylloscopus humei*; Newbiggin, Northumberland, 10th Feb. (one)
316. **Radde's Warbler**, *Phylloscopus schwarzi*; Wells, Norfolk, 16th Oct. (one)
317. **Dusky Warbler**, *Phylloscopus fuscatus*; Thorpness, Suffolk, 1st Nov. (one)
318. **Western Bonelli's Warbler**, *Phylloscopus bonelli*; Land's End, Cornwall, 29th Oct. (one)
319. **Wood Warbler**, *Phylloscopus sibilatrix*; Great Yarmouth, Norfolk, 26th April (one); Stiffkey, Norfolk, 22nd Aug. (one); St Mary's, I. o. Scilly, 9th Oct. (one)
320. **Chiffchaff**, *Phylloscopus collybita*; common
321. **Siberian Chiffchaff**, *Phylloscopus tristis*; Newbiggin, Northumberland, 10th Feb. (one); Blakeney Point, Norfolk,

3rd May (one)
322. Willow Warbler, *Phylloscopus trochilus*; common
323. Goldcrest, *Regulus regulus*; frequent
324. Firecrest, *Regulus ignicapillus*; several; Norfolk, Dorset, I. o. Scilly
325. Spotted Flycatcher, *Muscicapa striata*; frequent
326. Red-breasted Flycatcher, *Ficedula parva*; Wells, Norfolk, 28th Aug. & 12th Sep. (one); Weybourne, Norfolk, 16th Sep. (one)
327. Pied Flycatcher, *Ficedula hypoleuca*; frequent
328. Bearded Tit, *Panurus biarmicus*; frequent in Norfolk
329. Long-tailed Tit, *Aegithalos caudatus*; frequent
330. Marsh Tit, *Parus palustris*; several; Norfolk, Beds., Co. Durham
331. Willow Tit, *Parus montanus*; several near Fakenham, Norfolk
332. Crested Tit, *Parus cristatus*; Abernethy Forest, Invernesshire, 9th Feb. (three)
333. Coal Tit, *Parus ater*; frequent
334. Blue Tit, *Parus caeruleus*; common
335. Great Tit, *Parus major*; common
336. Nuthatch, *Sitta europaea*; frequent
337. Treecreeper, *Certhia familiaris*; frequent
338. Golden Oriole, *Oriolus oriolus*; Lakenheath, Suffolk, 17th May (four)
339. Red-backed Shrike, *Lanius collurio*; Hunstanton, Norfolk, 28th Aug. & 1st Sep. (one); Lizard, Cornwall, 3rd Sep. (one)
340. Great Grey Shrike, *Lanius excubitor*; Thursley Common, Surrey, 21st Feb. (one)
341. Woodchat Shrike, *Lanius senator*; St Leven, Cornwall, 25th March (one)

342. Jay, *Garrulus glandarius*; frequent
343. Magpie, *Pica pica*; frequent
344. Chough, *Pyrrhocorax pyrrhocorax*; Strumble Head, Pembrokeshire, 3rd Jan. (two)
345. Jackdaw, *Corvus monedula*; common
346. Rook, *Corvus frugilegus*; common
347. Carrion Crow, *Corvus corone*; common
348. Hooded Crow, *Corvus cornix*; frequent; N. Scotland, SW Ireland
349. Raven, *Corvus corax*; frequent
350. Starling, *Sturnus vulgaris*; common
351. Rose-coloured Starling, *Sturnus roseus*; Great Yarmouth, Norfolk, 24th Jan. (one); St Just, Cornwall, 29th Oct. (one)
352. House Sparrow, *Passer domesticus*; common
353. Tree Sparrow, *Passer montanus*; several; Norfolk, Rutland, Lincs.
354. Chaffinch, *Fringilla coelebs*; common
355. Brambling, *Fringilla montifringilla*; frequent
356. Serin, *Serinus serinus*; Sidcup, Greater London, 3rd March (one)
357. Greenfinch, *Carduelis chloris*; common
358. Goldfinch, *Carduelis carduelis*; common
359. Siskin, *Carduelis spinus*; frequent
360. Linnet, *Carduelis cannabina*; frequent
361. Twite, *Carduelis flavirostris*; frequent
362. Redpoll, *Carduelis cabaret*; frequent
363. Arctic Redpoll, *Carduelis hornemanni*; Titchwell, Norfolk, 28th Jan. (one)
364. Mealy Redpoll, *Carduelis flammea*; Titchwell, Norfolk, 28th Jan. (four)
365. Two-barred Crossbill, *Loxia leucoptera*; Bole, Yorkshire,

The List

2nd Sep. (one); Sandringham, Norfolk, 9th & 11th, Dec.(one)
366. Common Crossbill, *Loxia curvirostra*; frequent
367. Scottish Crossbill, *Loxia scotica*; Grantown, Invernesshire, 9th Feb. (five)
368. Common Rosefinch, *Carpodacus erythrinus*; Weybourne, Norfolk, 31st May & 3rd June (one)
369. Bullfinch, *Pyrrhula pyrrhula*; frequent
370. Hawfinch, *Coccothraustes coccothraustes*; regular at Sandringham, Norfolk
371. White-throated Sparrow, *Zonotrichia albicollis*; Flamborough Head, Yorks., 23rd Oct. (one)
372. Lapland Bunting, *Calcarius lapponicus*; Holkham, Norfolk, 21st Jan. (one); Fair Isle, Shetland, 23rd Sep. (one); Tresco, I. o. Scilly, 10th Oct. (one)
373. Snow Bunting, *Plectrophenax nivalis*; regular; Holkham, Norfolk. All winter
374. Yellowhammer, *Emberiza citronella*; frequent
375. Cirl Bunting, *Emberiza cirlus*; Exminster, Devon, 2nd Feb. (one)
376. Ortolan Bunting, *Emberiza hortulana*; Tore Common, Cornwall, 3rd Sep. (three)
377. Rustic Bunting, *Emberiza rustica*; St Mary's, I.o.Scilly, 5th Oct. (one)
378. Little Bunting, *Emberiza pusilla*; Atwick, Yorkshire, 23rd Oct. (one)
379. Reed Bunting, *Emberiza schoeniclus*; frequent
380. Corn Bunting, *Miliaria calandra*; frequent. Norfolk, Outer Hebrides
381. Bobolink, *Dolichonyx oryzivorus*; Hengistbury Head, Dorset, 2nd Nov. (one)

Butterflies

Silver-studded Blue
Plebejus argus spp. *argus* (L.)

White Admiral
Limenitis camilla (L.)

Camberwell Beauty,
Aglais (=*Nymphalis*) *antiopa* (L.)

Speckled Wood
Pararge aegeria spp. *insula* (Godart)

Burren Grayling
Hipparchia semele spp. *clarensis* de Lattin

Irish Grayling
Hipparchia semele ssp. *hibernica* Howarth

Isles of Scilly Meadow Brown
Maniola jurtina ssp. *cassiteridum* Graves

Irish Meadow Brown
Maniola jurtina ssp. *iernes* Graves

Other books by Brambleby Books

British and Irish Butterflies
The complete Identification, Field and Site Guide to the Species, Subspecies and Forms

Adrian Riley

This lavishly illustrated butterfly book is the first to cover all the adult forms found in the British Isles, including subspecies, written by a highly experienced lepidopterist.

The clear directions and field tips, with added OS grid references, will assist you in finding the butterflies and also in identifying them in their habitats, guided by details of behaviour and morphology. The text is complemented with over 270 photographs of live specimens in the field of all the taxa in full colour.

Paperback 352pp   ISBN: 978-0-9553928-0-1   £ 35.00

Bird Words
Poetic images of wild birds

Hugh D. Loxdale

"*A paperback of poems by a poet and professional biologist, reminding us that wild birds continue to inspire and delight in a host of different ways.*" Rob Hume, RSPB

Paperback 80 pp.   978-0-9543347-3-4   £5.99

UK500: Birding in the Fast Lane

James Hanlon

"*The Fast Lane is a highly pleasurable read…*" Jon Carter, *BirdWatch*

Paperback 136 pp.   978-0-9543347-8-9   £9.99

Feathers and Eggshells
The Bird Journal of a Young London Girl

Natalie Lawrence

"*I absolutely loved everything about this book and only wish that it had been around to inspire me as a young teenager.*" Jenny Steel, www.haiths.com

Hardback 72 pp. 978-0-9543347-7-2   £15.50

All books at special discount at
www.bramblebybooks.co.uk